# Economy of Words

## A guide to the words, workings and failures of a modern economy

*by worker bee*

## Julian Dorey

# Contents

# Introduction

Words that describe the workings of an economy can often take on a life of their own. When you think of the word 'economy' in any other context you would be drawn to descriptions of it's meaning like frugal, cheap or making the most of, for instance. Yet our economy could be more accurately described as the opposite, excessive, expensive and wasteful. It's partly this disconnect between traditional definitions of words and their morphed and manipulated meanings within the subject of economics that this book is about.

In a world where the economy and finance are so important, we should all have a basic understanding of the language that is used, and the way it's structured. In this book, I am examining the economy and the use of the basic language from which we can then gain some insight to what is really going on.

About three years ago I set out to learn about investing, but assumed I already knew enough about economics to get by. People buy and sell, money is made and invested, how difficult could that be?

As it turned out, it was far more complex and interesting than I had thought. Investing is hazardous, bank policy is opaque and without knowledge, the system as a whole seems very difficult to understand. But economic theory and language is where we can see some simple truths within this complexity. These truths however need a little effort to uncover.

My reading and research gave me a new level of insight into our economy, the winners, losers and issues around money. Instead of letting this information spin round in my head, I decided to write it down with the intention of making a book or maybe a Youtube video from it.

I set out to put down in words, the things that troubled me. I was disturbed by what I had learned and this I think is why I needed to write it down, to test it in physical form and to get it out of my head.

I don't know if authors normally write an intro first, but I wrote one early on to describe what I thought troubled me. That intro doesn't appear in this book. As I wrote and crystallised ideas and threads came together, I realised that the thing I thought I was troubled by, wasn't it at all. What I now realise is the thing, the essence of what I consider the main problem with our economy isn't money, it's wealth.

Not the wealth gap per see, or that according to Oxfam the richest 1% of people in the world own as much wealth as the remaining 99%. And just 8 individuals have a fortune as large as half of all the wealth in the world. These are troubling and very probably wrong. What I now believe is the main weakness in our economy is that we have mostly lost sight of how wealth is created in the first instance, and that so few people in Britain are actually employed doing this essential thing. Creating wealth means creating new money and new prosperity.

Our country is now trying to live off relatively few wealth creators and as that continues to prove insufficient, we are then forced to rely on ever increasing levels of debt to make up the difference. Wealth, money, tax and debt are the keys to understanding where our economy is today and where we are heading in the future.

Modern Britain definitely needs an economic reboot and I would like to see that lead by politicians but they have, for now, chosen a different path. They choose to 'pretend and extend' as the saying goes. They pretend that things are OK, that they are in control and therefore, there's nothing to worry about and they can extend their policies without limit. Because of this, when the reboot comes, it will be that much more chaotic than may otherwise have been necessary.

A reshaping of an economy will only come about in one of four ways, foreign military invasion, internal revolution, major structural reform or complete economic collapse. Three of these don't sound so tasty so what about structural reform.

Britain became the richest and most powerful country in the world during the industrial revolution. Internal changes to our technology, economic and legal structures lead to massive internal wealth creation. This lead to external expansion, exporting our goods, culture and political systems to other countries and regions (we can all have a view on how beneficial that was for the affected countries). This expansionary stage lead to massive wealth transfer from the countries we exported to, and extracted from, back to Britain.

This advantage never lasts. Other countries went through internal restructuring of different types. Roosevelt's 'new deal' policy dragged the USA out of the post depression period by building roads, bridges and dams in a Keynesian spending spree (more on Keynes later). Lending money and industry to the Germans and Britain during the second world war reset the American economy to be the biggest manufacturing country in the world. At the end of the war, they used this internal wealth creation to expand into the rest of the world with an export lead programme and the Marshall plan.

Other countries like Russia, China and Cuba have tried internal revolution. Their revolutions lead to the imposition of a communist system that lead to massive loss of wealth and lives. This ensured that these countries struggled to expand outwards except during the aftermath of war. Eventually internal restructuring has lead to some wealth creation and expansion, in China at least, as they have adopted a more capitalist style economic system.

China is now wealthy by many measures and are expanding their influence by exporting goods and an expansion of their military. This has come just at the time when Europe and the USA are at their weakest state for decades. We no longer create sufficient wealth and are living of the income of the future through debt accumulation. This is particularly true for Britain, USA and the southern states of Europe.

We desperately need an internal restructuring to reverse the effects of the last one. The liberalisation of labour and financial laws in the early '80s has left us with a seemingly busy work force that, I would suggest, lacks the fundamental ability to create sufficient wealth within our economy to justify our standard of living. We have a massive, and growing trade deficit and we have a massive debt burden that also now appears to be growing again.

The changes introduced by Maggie and Ronnie have changed our economies from production to consumption which caused public and private debts to sky rocket. The crashes of 1988, 2001 and 2008 should have been enough to demonstrate that something is very wrong with this structure. I think it's now clear that the banks and financial markets have an undue sway on our country and they are not going to change things voluntarily. Our reset needs to put banks and finance to work for us, not the other way round.

This book is intended to give an overview of economics in an easy and intelligible way (as far as that's possible). It's aimed at people who have no economics training or in depth knowledge, but who, like me want to know more than is offered by other sources. I examine the meaning of the words and workings of the institutions involved in our economy in an attempt to allow insight regarding what we are told by political, media and business leaders.

I concentrate mostly on the economies of the UK and USA but economics is both a universal and highly specific subject so the words are fairly common but the conditions in every country vary wildly.

Economics isn't really a science, economies are far too stochastic (liable to wild fluctuation) to test easily. Another problem is that it isn't possible to test economic theory in a scientific manner as we can't have a control to see what effect any changes to policy will make. The varying conditions, population, resources and geographic location of countries means that every case is a very unique situation. Because of this, there are very few things we can say are true about economics. You can only say something is 'true' if you control the boundaries of the question. For instance -

$$£2 + £2 = £4$$

We can say that this is true as all the information is within the sum, however if we change one small thing, the answer becomes very complex.

$$£2 + \$2 = ?$$

We have now introduced what economists would call, an 'externality'. To solve this sum we would need to decide the currency we want expressed in the answer and the current conversion rate. This means we would have to rely on foreign exchange traders (FOREX) over whom we have no control. Any answer obtained would be 'true' for just that moment as the exchange rate continues to change over time. This is why economics is so hard to use as a predictive tool, there are far too many externalities like commodity pricing, population changes and major events like wars that can affect any modern trading economy.

The fact that economics isn't a science also tends to allow economic theories or dogmas (opinion trading as fact) to out last their usefulness as you can't 'prove' them wrong. Recent experience though should tell us that the people in charge of our economy are probably following the wrong path.

When I listen to the news or documentaries about financial matters with my new, basic understanding of economics, it strikes me how little I used to know and how easy it was for my opinions to be manipulated by policy makers and the media. The media are not reliable in presenting the full story on economic issues and you can be sure the politicians will do all they can to pretend and extend.

> "You need economics if you are going to pick through the daily avalanche of misinformation and spot the spin. Without economics you can vote but you are really disenfranchised. You will be an innocent, subject to manipulation by vested interests using economic smoke and mirrors to pull the wool over your eyes. Without a grasp of economics you will be bemused by the contradictory statistics that spin doctors throw at you. Media coverage is often grossly misleading"
>
> *Vicky Pryce from "It's the Economy Stupid - Economics for Voters"*

Without understanding basic economics you will not notice their omissions and lies. As trader Allesio Rastani says, mainstream media provides 'news for the masses, not for the classes'. We get the news filtered for us and it's important to see beyond that filter.

I hope this book short cuts you to a realisation that all is not well with our economy and that only knowledge can help protect you against the crises and crashes. Only knowledge can inform a democratic choice and this same knowledge may also help you take an active interest in your own finances.

I also hope this book entertains. Despite the feeling of foreboding these introductory words contain, I don't want this to be a gloomy tale. There is plenty of things to be grateful for and to be optimistic about. When you get a new sports car, you need to know it can crash, but it's still a sports car. I just want a better driver, a more powerful engine under the bonnet and much, much better brakes all round.

# Words

I listened to a linguist being interviewed on the radio some years ago where he suggested that one of the reasons that english speaking countries did so well in the commercial world is the sheer breadth of the english language itself. Imagine you have a product or service you wish to sell into a competitive market. To test this you offer samples to friends and strangers alike and ask for feedback. The english language offers so many layers of subtle nuance, we can, with some effort, describe in fine detail what it is we like or dislike about our experiences with that product. This affords the developer of products a very accurate guide to where they are winning or losing in their market. Many languages have far fewer adjectival words to draw on and this itself gave english a competitive advantage. If a language has only 'like' or 'dislike' as descriptive words it will be very hard to create world beating products as this means all or nothing.

I like this concept, I like words.

This book is intended to give a straightforward guide to how our economy works by investigating the words, workings and failures of the UK economy. It's not authoritative, I am not an economist, I am a worker bee in the greater economy, looking for answers to why it just doesn't work very well for everyone. Therefore this book also has some political undertones, not intended explicitly (except the Gordon Brown stuff) but unavoidable when dealing with this politicised subject.

I have put headings on each word or phrase that I want to describe but they aren't in alphabetical order like a glossary (although you can refer to the index to move quickly to a description when required). I want the book to have a narrative of sorts, so that words can be described in context with one another in a more logical way, not prescribed by the alphabet.

## Youtube content.

Some years ago I read Lance Armstrong's biography, "It's not about the bike" which I enjoyed all the more as I was able to watch excerpts from his races on youtube as I read. I found this a really interesting, mixed media experience and I want this book to have that feel (without the drugs or lycra).

I have included links to several videos within this book which I highly recommend watching as you come across them in the text. I found youtube a highly educational resource and the videos I have chosen have some world authorities on economics presenting their views which have also helped to shape the content of this book.

In the investing world, almost any written recommendation or company profile will include the disclaimer – 'DO YOUR OWN RESEARCH' (DYOR) and this is true for this book as well. Never take the first account or opinion of what is 'true' with economics. Truth is always relative to the lens through which the commentator looks.

**Thanks to Dominic Frisby for his fantastic books, 'Life after the state' and 'Bitcoin'. If I can hit the target as well as he did, I will be more than satisfied**

# A quick start courtesy of money supply and the Greek debt crisis

I'm not a patient person. If a book doesn't grab me in 30 pages, It's dead to me. I want to grab your attention and give you a flavour of what this book is about right now.

Please imagine a small country with a money supply (total of money in the economy) of 20 million units. The island nation has a beautiful house on the top of a hill overlooking the bay, it's fantastic. No matter how fantastic it is, it would be impossible for you to pay anywhere near 20 million units for it as this would require extracting all the available money out of the economy, which is impossible. With such a limited money supply, the most you could spend on this property would be a small fraction of the total, let's say the highest market price could be 100,000 units.

The island found this limited money supply a bit restricting, so they printed an additional 180 million units to boost the money supply to 200 million units. Now, by the same logic, the best house on the island could sell for a lot more, perhaps as much as 10 million units. Has the house become more valuable?

There are two sides to every trade but we are coached into seeing just one, often the wrong one. We are coached to see our unit of currency as the constant, not the variable. The value of the beautiful house on the island hasn't really changed, only the amount of currency we need to express its premium has changed. The value of the property hasn't changed, it's the value of the currency that has decreased. It's the value of the currency decreasing over time as the number of units expands that creates the illusion of a rising house price. Both sides can be true, but we only see one.

Foreign exchange markets (Forex) are an area where like for like comparison forces a layer of truth. On the news you may hear that the pound falls against the dollar, or the pound gains against the euro. You would never hear that the pound loses value as house prices have risen again. This is a truth, just not the one we are encouraged or coached to see.

Who got bailed out in the Greek debt crisis? Do you think it was the Greeks? There are two sides to every trade and in the case of the bailout it was actually the bond holders who got bailed out, not the Greeks. When the banks get 'bailed out', they get lots of free money to spend on themselves, past errors and crimes are forgiven, bonuses are paid and it's back to business as usual. Does that sound like the type of 'bail out' the Greeks received?

What actually happened was the IMF forced an unrepayable loan onto the Greeks to ensure primarily American, German, French and Italian banks didn't suffer a total loss that could have sparked yet another banking crisis. They are hoping that european banks and legislators have been bought enough time to sort themselves out before Greece goes bust again. In a rational market, no one would have loaned Greece that money.

Of course both sides of these examples of manipulated understanding are sort of true-ish. As mentioned before, it's almost impossible to call any statement about the economy 'true' as simple statements don't do justice to the complexity of these systems.

You would do well to bear this test in mind whenever you are given news about the economy. How true can this news be and who is on the other side of the trade?

## Video 1 - 11 mins. A bit cheesy but worth a watch.

Youtube search - What banks don't want you to know about the Greek crisis

https://youtu.be/nSMfDbzkCOw

# Why me, why now?

I was born in 1963, the end of the 'baby boomer' generation, into a UK economy that was, by all accounts, the sick man of Europe. Our family voted conservative. We watched 'The Money Programme', serious news, listened to radio 4 and had broadsheet newspapers on the weekend. My father always considers himself working class but we had a good home which my parents owned, my parents were employed but eventually they started a small business and we enjoyed a decent standard of living.

I count myself very fortunate to have been born when and where I was, I have seen the UK economy transformed and have enjoyed the prosperity of our time. The last thirty years have changed so much for our family and for most people in the UK because of the changes introduced in the early to mid eighties. So why am I now questioning the legitimacy of those changes and what the actual drivers of the economy really are?

I became interested in learning about investing because of my pension. I have worked hard and saved into my pension plan, the first of which I started when I was 23. My wife, Julia has done the same. A few years ago we put our respective pensions into a new scheme, the Self Invested Pension Plans (SIPP) so we could buy a commercial property into which I moved the business that I had bought from my father. This property then created a rental income for us to invest. Julia chose to invest her cash balances in funds chosen by our advisor, but I decided that I wanted to be in charge of my own pension investments and although I had done some share trading in the past, I wanted to learn as much as I could before taking on this responsibility.

I read quite a few books on share trading, which were mostly interesting and I certainly learned a lot, but it was an impulse buy that has lead me to learn about the economy, money and the politics behind economists. I bought a 'recommended for you' book on my Kindle called 'Confessions of an economic hit man' by John Perkins. It's a really interesting book with a great title.

Hitman outlined the way the USA uses financial institutions, bribery, revolution, assassination and war to further their political and economic agenda and it was a real eye opener. This lead me to read more about economics and less about shares which suddenly seemed a bit boring.

It was in 'Death of Money' by Jim Rickards that I was introduced to what 'money' really is. Now it was all starting to come together. Imagine not ever thinking about or understanding money! But that is the truth for most of us since we accept money as it is and haven't really considered that it needs questioning. Money is money. I didn't have a clue before and this book is my attempt to shortcut as many people as possible to the same realisation of what money really is and how it interacts with us and forms the economy.

Economics is, in many ways, pretty simple to understand, but obviously the difficult part initially is understanding terminology. Once I understood the language and the interrelationships, it became quite easy to think about the economy and have an opinion on what I was being told by the media's favoured economic spokesman.

The chosen spokesman has an incredibly powerful influence on how we see the economy, it's faults and possible solutions. The dominant economic doctrine of our time is the neo-liberal consensus. This is a Keynesian style doctrine which insists that government intervention is good and particularly necessary to provide stimulus in times of economic stress. This doctrine is currently the underlying premiss for media debate but with a little effort you can find very credible, and qualified economists who can give an alternate view. They aren't usually invited to give commentary on Sky news or the BBC so you will need to check out the 'alt' media scene. Professor Steve Keen is very interesting and Professor Hu Jong Chan's book, '23 things they don't tell you about capitalism' is a refreshing look at the other side of the story. There are two sides to every trade and every story. These economics professors are examples of people who can give an alternative view.

**Video 2 - 11 mins.**

Youtube search RSA animate - Economics is for everyone.
https://youtu.be/NdbbcO35arw?list=PLD7u4sAYcu8qZc2JbDTX_cc28siMUoNOo

Although economics is relatively simple in absolute terms, unfortunately there is a motivation for economists to make it all sound very difficult. In the same way as lawyers use extremely contrived modes of language to write a simple agreement in order to protect their jobs (as only another lawyer understands twisted legalese). Economists also like their subject to seem quite opaque in order to preserve theirs.

Don't be fooled.

The business of professional economists is guiding, modelling or predicting the future course of the economy. This is a very difficult thing to do, as we have seen over many years. Peter Schiff, a US based financier and blogger, said a very interesting thing about economics. He made the point that we seem to be unable to learn from economic history. We don't start our mathematical, architectural or scientific knowledge from scratch every few years, we build on the work of previous generations. In economics we seem to forget what gets us into trouble and just repeat the same mistakes over and over. In economics, we don't 'stand on the shoulders of giants' as Isaac Newton (former Master of the Royal Mint as well as physicist) once said.

Mike Malloney of GoldandSilver.com believes that the long term debt cycle is around 70-100 years, precisely because it takes a generation of people, made cautious by financial calamity to die out, before the next generation emerges without these negative memories and repeats all the same things that caused the last crash.

We have seen so many booms and busts and all of them have a very similar path although they aren't identical. Bubbles have been seen in economies around the world, the tulip bubble in Holland in the 1630's is an interesting case in point. The beautiful tulips brought to Holland at that time were so popular, so sought after that the price for a single bulb could be more than a year's income for most people. It was during this time that the futures market was introduced as people bid on next year's increased bulb supply. Too much money flooding into a non productive commodity chasing a finite supply, herding, over exuberance, mania. Eventually a blight hit the tulip crop and the bubble burst, huge amounts were lost. Tulips – houses; tulips – shares; tulips – derivatives. Where will the next bubble be?

Gordon Brown was very keen on his mantra 'no more boom and bust'. He said it in the house of commons more than 100 times. What did he produce? Yep! a boom followed by an almighty bust in 2007/8. It's true to say that the global financial crisis started in the USA with the subprime crisis but this was a symptom of the lax regulation and non supervision of financial markets encouraged by Gordon Brown and Ben Bernanke. Too much money chasing non-productive, risky derivatives. Herding, mania, kaboooom!

Economics cannot be easily separated from politics. Macro economics (economics of a big thing like a country) is inherently political and its theories are dominated by big names like Marx, Keynes, Hayek and Friedman. If you are a Marxist, you are of the left, Friedman, of the right and so on. Economics is seen through a lens of economic and therefore political theory. Micro economics (economics of a small thing like a business or household) is not really a political thing, it's about survival.

As stated before, I was brought up as a conservative and I still am broadly sympathetic to the right of politics as I believe in liberty and the market mechanism. After a lot of thought however, I'm unsure whether I can ever vote conservative again unless they change their monetary policy substantially. Democracy should be about choice but our main political parties are all following the same, neo liberal economic policies.

# Tomatoes and wetsuits – innovation and globalisation

I can remember the early seventies a bit and although this period is reasonably fashionable now, at the time it was mostly rubbish. As children, we had a massive amount of freedom and very few distractions, which was a great start to life. But the problem with the seventies was that nothing worked very well, if at all. Constant strikes, the three day week, the oil crisis, nationalised industries and a command economy. Britain in the early seventies was probably as communist as Russia or China are today. We were the sick man of Europe and it sort of felt that way as well.

A lot of the problem was that we lived in a command economy, meaning the government had a very large role in deciding what was made and sold. They owned a lot of large industries such as steel and coal and didn't allow free markets to work. The European and world markets weren't established as they are now. Citizens weren't yet consumers in the modern sense as there was little choice and not much disposable income. We mostly made do with the limited choices and had a fairly limited diet in comparison to today.

When I accompanied my mother to the shops we had a choice of local grocers, butchers, bakers. The choices were limited, the produce was mostly seasonal but basic. Tomatoes were orangey, mid sized bullets. Salads were comprised of limp lettuce, cucumber and possibly celery and then sliced tomato. I don't miss the seventies.

Somewhere around '74 our families shopping habits started to change as a Mace store opened in our local town. This was a small supermarket where things were stacked on open shelves and you walked all the way around to fill your own basket (some of the baskets were big, and had wheels!). A few years later a Waitrose opened as well, now we were in the big league. More choices, more convenience but not much change to the tomatoes.

I would say that it wasn't until late nineties that I first saw tomatoes 'on the vine'. It seemed a bit odd but what a revolution, they actually tasted nice, all the time. We bought them and we continued to buy them when available. In other words, we preferred them to their more solid cousin and were happy to pay the premium price they commanded. This simple decision, repeated all over the country, guided tomato producers to follow this new direction within their business. Now in my local store we can choose from several named varieties of premium tomatoes, big ones, small ones, on the vine, different colours and they are all great.

To me, this is as good an example of the visibly competitive market economy as you can get. Some nameless tomato grower innovated the delivery of tomatoes to the consumer by leaving them on the vine. I'm sure there were also many unseen innovations to tomato varieties as well as improvements in pesticides, irrigation, picking, factory style green housing, handling and packaging materials.

This is the power of an economy guided by visible consumer choice, the 'invisible hand' that steers our industries to innovate and compete for our custom. We should be proud of the choice of tomatoes open to us. Well done, we choose innovation, we all made this happen. If there can be this much innovation to the humble tomato, what else can the visibly competitive market economy achieve?

I am lucky enough to live close to what must be one of the most beautiful beaches in England - Bantham in south Devon. I go there often and I see a massive difference to the beaches of my youth. Not the beach per se, but the amount of 'stuff' people have with them. Wetsuits everywhere, pop up tents as well as wind breaks, all sorts of inflatable things.

A wetsuit clad person used to be intent on going diving or possibly windsurfing but now lots of normal beach goers choose to don the neoprene for leisure swimming. The suits have definitely got better, more flexible and lighter and crucially, a lot cheaper.

The Thatcher revolution changed things radically and eventually we became a consumer society, probably around the mid nineties, but this has really taken off since the internet has become a common part of our lives. The internet was really kicking off at the same time as China was emerging as a major manufacturing economy. If a business wants to cut costs to gain a competitive advantage, one of the ways they can do that is to produce their goods in a country where labour is cheaper, like China. The humble wetsuit has become affordable in two ways, the price is lower and, partly due to globalisation, we have more disposable income.

These two forces, innovation and globalisation are crucial to our current economy and have driven companies forward in producing better, cheaper and far more numerous product choices. Access to cheaper markets for commodities and manufactured goods have pretty much killed inflation as we can buy better stuff cheaper year on year. You can buy a 60" TV now for less than £700, where as10 years ago a 50" TV was £5,000.

There is little doubt that up until recently, globalisation has improved living standards in the developed countries. But we are now in a period where voters all over the world are questioning the direction of globalisation and what the costs and benefits really are. Many people in the developing world are 'exploited' by the manufacturing industries supplying western markets and the low skilled workers in developed countries have seen no real increase in incomes for years because their jobs have gone or wages are suppressed to stay competitive with countries like China and India. Politicians like Donald Trump, Berni Saunders and Jeremy Corbyn are promoting far more protectionist policies than we have seen in the last thirty years because the people directly suffering from globalisation, and those politically sympathetic to their plight, have grown into a very large constituency.

Interesting times.

So let's get into some words. I have tried to arrange these words in an order that has some narrative. Any word that has a section devoted to it is in italics, You can find it via the index or, most likely it's coming up shortly.

# Wealth

What is wealth? That's a philosophical question of sorts as many people would make the case that certain lifestyles or experiences can give us wealth and I wouldn't disagree.

As I am trying to write a book on economics though, I only want to make the distinction between real monetary wealth creation, the rent seekers who feed on it and the illusion of asset price inflation.

There are essentially only two drivers of economic wealth creation, natural and human resources, both of which can be used wisely or wasted.

For the whole history of man as a species, we have been moving our technology forward in pursuit of more ways we can use natural resources. When you consider the way our ages of man are described, they also reflect this progression. Stone age, Iron, bronze and then surely coal and steam, steel, oil, and silicone.

As our technology and sciences improve we are able to find more ways of exploiting natural resources and bring them into the economic sphere. At one time, oil was considered a nuisance because it could contaminate good land and had absolutely no use at all. Then enter a new technology that is developed to exploit the black stuff, and the rest, as they say, is history. Our history is a progressive increase in the exploitation of natural resources.

Human resources, and the division of labour.

Adam Smith describes how the division of labour has allowed people working together to create a 'surplus', which is yet another way of saying profit. In his book 'Wealth of Nations' he uses pin making as an example of how innovation and cooperation allows workers in well organised teams to easily outperform the efforts of people working alone. By reducing the production down to its elements and giving each element to an individual, a massive increase in production can be created. Each person, only having to master one task, can truly become a master of it, and not only is the quality of their work better, it's also faster. A lone pin maker may only make 15-20 pins in a day, whereas team of ten can make thousands per day.

A surplus in this context means that, through efficient working, you are creating more money than you need to live. This surplus money can then be invested in something else without adversely affecting your standard of living.

When feudal societies lived off the land and were generally very poor, ordinary people were unable to easily create a useable surplus. As our ancestors moved out of the countryside and towards the towns and cities, they came together to create very early industry. The economic benefits of the division of labour are easy to see and the surplus created is real wealth. Real wealth is created through us working to create a surplus through the use of technology, cooperation and invention.

We now have a very developed, sort of free market world where many sectors are in an equilibrium. A mature market for goods and services always tend towards equilibrium where prices are stable and demand and supply also tend towards being equal.

This equilibrium state rarely produces a large surplus within visibly competitive businesses. Disruptive technology and innovation can give a mature market a new shake up which gives opportunity to innovators to make money. If your production is improved by technology to become 50% more efficient and the market price remains the same you will make loads of new wealth.

An alternative route to increasing wealth creation is to move your production to a different sector, or actually create a new sector where a price equilibrium hasn't been established. On the vine tomatoes, iPods, Dyson cleaners and Wonderbras for instance, a successful sector shift gives the possibility to make lots of new wealth as well.

This is the essential role of the entrepreneur. They have to marshal the available capital inputs like human resources, machinery, technology, suppliers and money, and use these with invention and innovation to create a product or service they can sell into a market at a profit. When entrepreneurs are outnumbered by bureaucrats and rent seekers ('elf and safety etc) a country is heading towards trouble as only entrepreneurs have the ability to create the conditions for new wealth creation.

There are two sides to every trade, so although people working together can create a surplus, to be effective this also requires other people who have the means and desire to pay for the goods that they are selling. Our consumerist society is necessary in so far as all products need a market, but if the market is restricted to only our most basic needs, little trade will ensue. It's the market for fripperies and impulse purchases that truly makes the world go around by providing wealth creation opportunity. That's kinda sad, but true nonetheless

Social working practices in factories, kitchens, studios and workshops can create a surplus, and nowadays technology can help us create a surplus too. Machines, CAD/CAM, robotics, the interweb and big data can all help us to create a surplus.

Surplus created in these ways can be short lived though as the market price mechanism will reduce the price to reflect the latest production methods, the surplus will then disappear or at least greatly reduce. Efficient and less efficient workers then have to fight for market share and innovate and improve their production techniques yet again to re establish a surplus. The most inefficient and unpopular businesses will be put out of business and their capital (staff and machines etc) will be re allocated to more successful enterprises. This basic price/innovation mechanism is why a broadly capitalist society will always duff up a state socialist society. State socialists will protect and regulate before they innovate, just think about the French and you'll get the picture.

Creating a surplus of production through social working patterns became the basis of the socialist doctrine. Socialists believe that as workers effectively create the wealth, they should also control the surplus and distribute it equally. They also believe that the control of the means of production should be democratic, that each worker should have an equal say in the management of their own labour. This system has so far failed to sustain innovation and create the competitive destruction required to stay ahead of competitors.

Partly because of this, a pure socialist theory has never proven to be sustainable in the long term all though most attempts have been corrupted by authoritarian rule. The Soviets made a complete mess of their country and economy, starving millions of it's citizenry TO DEATH. And yet, people still think socialism can work. To any theory you have to add human nature, and that normally throws a big old spanner in the works.

What we think of as socialism now is more state capitalism with income redistribution thrown in. It's a system designed for and supported by 'rent seekers', the class of people who are, paradoxically, totally divorced from social working principles. Think of the people who did really well under Gordon Brown and you will have the rent seekers in your sights. Administrators, bankers, 'elf and safety officers, health workers, councils and regulators. Not a single person in these roles can create a surplus. The rent seekers are living off of the surplus created by the worker bees. It doesn't mean they are bad people of course, far from it I hope, but they can't help us create wealth. These roles were incredibly rare in the times of Marx and Engels and I think they would be appalled by the behaviour of modern politicians who claim to be socialist.

Government needs to not only allow, but encourage business to create the new wealth that they can then redistribute through taxation. Modern 'socialism', as practised by Labour and Conservative governments, Democrat and Republican parties is failing so spectacularly because they have forgotten about the requirement to create a surplus. Politicians find it easier to borrow our future and the next generation's future earnings, whatever it takes for them to keep the game going. Pretend and extend.

In the way that socialism has only been tried out as state capitalism, we haven't seen capitalism given a go either since the last war. If we want to create a surplus again and close our trade deficit, put people in productive jobs, cut down on rent seekers and build a fairer society, we need to rediscover social working within capitalist markets.

The surplus capital created in social and technological working environments will then go looking for something to invest in. This is wealth that has been created and is inherently different to what we now see as wealth in 21st century Britain. A new way of banking and investing is needed to bring these changes around, as well as a whole lot of political will.

We now waste far too much of our human resources as we have lost sight of what real wealth is. The people who are getting rich today in the financial industry do not create wealth, they move wealth around and feed from it. Finance is a parasitic industry. In the financial industry, it takes a client of that industry to lose money, for another client of the industry to make money. Shares aren't really traded on the underlying value of the business, they are traded on the belief that some schmuck will buy them off me, for more than I paid for them. And nowadays, several nanoseconds later, some schmuck usually does.

No real wealth is created in this process. The vast salaries are skimmed off the real wealth, the wealth created in private competitive business using social and technological working practices. Finance extracts 'rents' from this wealth as it's moved around the system and are a tax on our labour.

The shear number of traders and volume of trades, creates the volatility that ensures maximum fee extraction. Of course, all this is lovely for the people in these industries but it's a mass misallocation of effort and talent.

We still have a considerable amount of real wealth creation in the UK, we have some amazing businesses, incredibly skilled workers and entrepreneurs but our fixation on the financial markets in the last 30 years has left us weaker than many competitors who haven't suffered as badly from this illusion as we have; South Korea, Japan, China, Vietnam, Germany, Switzerland....... Lots of successful countries with large manufacturing sectors creating real wealth. I hope we can join them again soon.


## Natural resources.

We live on a finite planet. However, our current money and consumption models don't fit easily with finite resources as we are fixed in a system which demands constant growth. Our natural resources are a source of great wealth but their allocation is also very mismanaged.

Our collective, human history has been a constant search for ways to exploit what is around us in our local environments. Before the industrial revolution and particularly, before the age of steam, we were pretty limited in our ability to move large quantities of materials any significant distances.

(A word about "exploit". This isn't necessarily a bad thing, the word gets a very bad press nowadays, but this is a little unfair as it can mean 'maximise the use of' which is a good thing. It doesn't have to mean waste or a corrupt use of people or things. Let's get exploit off the naughty step, at least a bit)

Since the age of steam and the rapid expansion of bulk trade, we've had the ability to move huge amounts of material around the world. Coal, ores of different kinds, oil of course, timber, wheat, bananas. You name it, we can shift it. The result has been that empires like ours and that of the USA have used far more natural resources than we really own. We have used conquest (war) and our military might to strip other countries of the natural resources, their natural wealth. In the developed west, we still consume vastly more material per capita than any countries in the developing and third worlds.

A distinction has to be made between those resources that are potentially sustainable like wheat or soft timber, and those that are finite like ores and oil. In each case though, it's time the west took a lot more responsibility for the amount we consume so that these resources can benefit the people of the countries from which they are extracted. America especially need to stop invading countries for oil and we need to stop supporting them.

# Markets

Markets are the basis of classical economics as first set out by Adam Smith in his book 'The Wealth of Nations'. Markets are essentially a price discovery mechanism, which means that in an open market, agents within that market can decide at what price goods or services will be bought and sold for. The action of the market will 'discover' what the current market price is, and the larger the market, the more accurate you can expect the pricing to be.

Consider 'on the vine' tomatoes and how much of a premium you would pay for them. The market works by having these decisions played out and setting the market price for a certain item. The market also has to deal with supply and demand, so a market that gets flooded with a certain item will generally see the price go down as suppliers compete for market share. Scarcity works in the opposite direction driving prices up.

So if on the vine tomatoes have a premium price already, and then there is unexpected scarcity the price will go up and there will be a price at which you would revert to their more solid and tasteless cousins. If a market price for the now scarce 'on the vine' tomatoes is set at £3 per 500 grams but normal tommies are only 80p for the same amount, many people will decide that the normal tomato is a more rational way to spend their money.

Markets can have several states usually dependant on the maturity of that market. Let's discount financial markets for now as they play by different rules. A market for regular, visibly competitive goods and services can start out erratic, become mature and then become liable to innovative and technological disruption.

Many economic theories will state that markets tend towards equilibrium where prices are relatively stable and the supply side and demand side are somewhat equal. In a state of equilibrium, prices can be affected by commodity or other input costs but otherwise remain within a predictable range. This does appear to be true for many things we consume but we also have hierarchical markets where a hair cut for me is £8.50 but for a beauty conscious person may pay £60 or more. There are a few barbers around where I live and £8.50 is the right sort of price. This is probably also true for the high end stylist.

So equilibrium doesn't mean a single market, but price stability within a market sector.

This equilibrium state will normally mean that most businesses within their sector are making modest margins, or margins similar to their piers.

Market equilibrium can last a long time and will wait for a new technology or innovation for a change of state. Uber has created a change of state in the taxi business. The market price has come down and regular taxis now look over priced. Fast food restaurants had a similar effect years ago but conversely fine dining has recently created a new, higher price market sector. Robotics and CAD/CAM are creating changes of state for manufacturing now. Markets tend to reach an equilibrium state in the absence of technological shift or between shifts.

The market is essentially a price discovery mechanism which many economists believe is a market where the price of an item for sale is weighed up by our rational minds and we choose to buy or not in a very sober way. Economists would describe this as 'maximising utility', ie maximising the usefulness of our money. This could be said to be true in many circumstances, but other factors, like emotions play an important role in our decision making. This is certainly true in financial markets, so we have to look at different mechanisms to understand markets fully.

Rational market theory has dominated economics in recent decades. In financial markets we hear phrases like, 'let the market decide' or 'all information is reflected in the price' as if all agents in the market are holding all the price related information and calculators.

But unlike haircuts, taxis and manufactured goods, we are buying and selling financial assets at megabit speed through intermediaries who we think of as expert in their field. Can we trust financial markets?

Daniel Kahneman is a behavioural psychologist who was awarded the Nobel prize for economics in 2002 for his work on our minds rational (and sometimes irrational) responses to problems. In his book 'Fast and Slow Thinking' he describes how our brain can be seen as two separate systems, the 'quick' brain always has an answer at hand, it's a mechanism that gets us out of trouble a lot of the time but it can also get us into trouble as well. The 'slow' part of our brain chooses to accept or reject this quick response.

He uses a simple problem to illustrate the cognitive illusion (mistake) our brains can make. Try this...........

A man buys a bat and a ball that together cost him $1.10. The bat costs $1 more than the ball. How much does the bat cost'

I suspect you're brain shouted out an answer for you.

Did you like the answer your brain offered?

Was it 10 cents? Or was it just 10.

Do you want to try that again with the slow thinking part of your brain?

Daniel Kahneman separates the brain into the fast part (system 1) and slow part (system 2). The fast system shouts out an answer straight away and it takes the slow, present and conscious part of your brain to test this answer to make sure it's right. The problem is that this requires work and we are, like it or not, inherently lazy.

He performed an experiment where he would chat to his students while walking along a path. During this chat he would drop in a little problem for his students to solve, He asked them to start at the number 100 and then count back by subtracting 7's. 100, 93, 86, 79.......and so on. All his students, some of America's brightest, had to stop walking to complete this task. This is a relatively simple computation, yet the brain got so busy on it, they could no longer put one foot in front of the other. This is the level of resistance we have to using system 2 and why we follow our more intuitive fast brain, (system 1) all too often.

Your quick thinking brain didn't hang around to really test the number it had come up with because system 2 is only applied when system 1 doesn't offer any sort of answer (in the case of a sum like 1289 x 756 for instance) or we spot a problem. The logic of the answer 10, supplied by system 1 was too strong consequently it was accepted by system 2. This is a cognitive illusion and Daniel Kahneman showed that we are also particularly susceptible to making these kinds of mistakes with money. He presents a theory where we are also all liable to certain biases that affect our decision making.

(The bat cost $1.05 and the ball was 5 cents. $1 difference)

We see in the financial markets how financial experts can make a lot of mistakes thus making the market inefficient and indicating that there are more than rational mechanisms at play. If the markets were indeed rational, they wouldn't jump around as much as they do. A 10 -30% shift in a share price in a single day is rarely 'rational'. It's predicated by two of our deepest emotions, greed and fear. If you have used your own money for some share dealing, you will have experienced these emotions, especially the fear.

Biases are more subtle than raw emotions but will still have a very important part in our decision making. Herding is a way of describing a social bias because we like to be among friends and seen to be part of the team. Herding has the effect of bidding up the price of popular shares as more people want to join in, and this can be an indicator of trouble ahead if the process goes into reverse.

### Video 3 - 52 Mins. Excellent video, well worth the time.

Youtube search - How money changes the way we think and behave.
https://youtu.be/3Gkq4n97ATc?list=PLD7u4sAYcu8qZc2JbDTX_cc28siMUoNOo

This video shows how our emotions and biases lead us to make very strange decisions like bidding $28 for a $20 note or how we price objects based on emotion.

Behavioural psychology has demonstrated the deep flaws in rational market theory. The fact that so many people fell for, and continue to believe in it, is a classic case of herding.

Daniel Kahneman follow up.

### Video 4 - 20 Mins

Search Youtube or TED - Daniel Kahneman: The riddle of experience vs. memory
https://youtu.be/XgRlrBl-7Yg

Daniel Ariely is also a brilliant speaker. Give him some of your time as well

Search youtube or TED - Are we in control of our decisions? Dan Ariely
https://youtu.be/9X68dm92HVI

# Free Markets

The term 'free' markets is another occasion where the meaning of words has morphed to accommodate the neoliberal agenda. Today, when free markets are discussed, the picture is one of competing markets without the encumbrance of regulation, tariffs and taxes. But we don't have free markets in this way, and we don't really want them. Honestly. Free markets are bad. What we want is regulated markets.

Economics Professor Michael Hudson was asked in a youtube interview about the modern concept of free markets. He referenced the high debt burden of most ordinary people creating a fairly passive workforce because of fears of losing their jobs, before saying-

"A free market is where the 1% get to smash the 99% without any ability of the 99% to fight back, a free market is where people do what they are told. A free market is the opposite of what Adam Smith A store of value: Tricky, but ignoring and John Stuart Mill and everyone else meant by 'free' market. The classical economists meant a market free from rentiers, free from landlords, free from banks where everyone got what they deserved and produced. But under Greenspan *(former governor of the US fed)* in modern economics, a market is free from government regulation, free from throwing the bankers in jail when they commit crime, free from any kind of policy making by government, by labour unions, by society. A free market today is a centrally planned economy but it's not planned by government, the planning is shifted out of government to the banks"

Government should regulate capitalists, without regulation, who knows what they will get up to. For instance if I wanted a 'Mad Max' car with spears and flames jutting out of it, finished with lead paint, lead petrol, no seat belts and made exclusively by pygmy slave labourers, this might seem a little eccentric but in a free market, I could get that.

What we already have are regulated markets and the goal should be towards equalising these regulations to make trade fair. The regulations should protect the consumer, the workforce and, hopefully the environment. But they should also protect small business from big business to avoid the inevitable formation of cartels and monopolies.

It's the regulations, mostly unseen, that set the market rules within which, we would want to see open trade without tariffs and with free and fair competition between companies and countries. Free trade should be shorthand for this scenario but do we have this now?

Definitely not. In the last twenty years it's been the developed countries that have been losing out in this free trade illusion (exceptions include farmers). Our manufacturers particularly have had the weight of regulation put upon them and have been asked to compete with countries without the same level of regulation. This cannot be seen as free trade when our regulated industry competes with child labour, workers being unfairly exploited, massive environmental damage both locally and exported through mass movement of goods.

China, India, Bangladesh and other players from the developing world have used lack of regulation and poverty wages, instead of innovation and technology to compete within markets, Their environments, especially that of China, has paid the price with terrible water and air pollution.

The irony of course, is that they may have to do this to develop. Britain was out of the industrial revolution starting blocks first, but we still used child labour, workers unfairly exploited, massive environmental damage both locally and exported through mass movement of goods.

The element the developing countries are now denied is protectionism. This policy can give local developing firms breathing space to develop and improve their working practices and technologies. A company in Gambia can't suddenly start making TVs for instance, at the world market price and quality as it's unlikely they could command the necessary capital, equipment and training to achieve this. If however they used trade protection measures like import taxes, then the local firm could be protected from world class TV manufacturers for a number of years, they can then use a home market monopoly to develop their production to a stage where barriers could be steadily lifted. Often developing companies buy obsolete production lines from developed countries to start this process as India did with car production. An Indian company now own Jaguar Land Rover and is a truly world class manufacturer.

The World Trade Organisation (USA/EU axis) is very mistrustful of barriers and tariffs which makes it very hard for developing countries to start new businesses that can compete with the equal regulations and standards we should be demanding.

The big corporates like the free trade regulations as they can flood unprotected markets with their goods which prevents competition developing. The IMF also helps to prevent developing countries actually develop by imposing free trade and their structural reform package, more on the IMF later.

Free trade is a bit of a myth sold to the masses, exploited by the classes.

# Consumers

Consumers play a very important role in the market mechanism. They help to drive industrial innovation and through their purchases of goods and services, help to create a surplus which can then re invested.

If no one is buying stuff, we'll be in the dark age again, so we need a mechanism to shift one person's surplus to another via trade. We therefore live in a consumerist society. I am a consumer. I would find it difficult to change, to give up all the 'stuff' I like to buy. I know I have to work hard to gain a surplus so that I can have the latest thing, (often new kitesurfing gear in my case).

The verb, to "consume" can mean to eat, drink etc. It can also mean consume as by fire or flood, to destroy, wipe out, or it can mean consume by emotion, destroy all other feeling by being consumed by fear or guilt.

To consume fundamentally means to destroy, (let's face it, you're not getting the food and drink back in an acceptable form either). Is destruction really a great model for a society? When you think about how we consume and destroy natural resources as we live our post industrial lives, it's great for us, the kindle owners, but for billions of others born into less affluent countries, things aren't working out so well.

We need to trade, but not in a way that is damaging to other societies. Can we have a system that has winners and winners rather than big winners and losers like our current situation?

This isn't our fault directly, but our nation states and supra national institutions haven't helped They have ensured we have maintained our advantages and subjugated countries and their resources to keep us on top, permanently they hope.

# Supply and demand

There are two sides to every trade, seller and buyer, supply and demand. The visibly competitive portion of our economy is guided by what Adam Smith referred to as 'the invisible hand'. This guiding hand would steer capital, or what we would probably refer to as profits, towards businesses that compete for, and win customers.

This process would increase business activity, innovation and living standards. We see this in the economy of supply led and demand led business growth.

## Demand

Tattoos are all over the place now, literally. When did this happen? Late '90s into the naughties. At some point public figures like footballers and singers were getting tattooed and many people decided they also wanted a tattoo. There weren't many tattooists around and the ones that were started to get busy. Prices went up, tattooists did well.

Due to the increased incomes and visibility of tattoo artists, new entrants came into the market and spread around the country. We now have a tattoo parlour in our local town. Prices settled, innovation and discounting follow which would help to boost demand again. These are the market forces. Watch out for a good business in the future, tattoo removal, it will be huge.

## Supply

Asparagus, and lots of it this year. I like fresh asparagus, a friend would give me some in good years but I didn't really buy it at the shops. This year, that changed. There was asparagus all over the shelves, it was cheap, really nice and fresh and I bought some, and then some more. I had limited idea what to do with it but I learned new ways to cook it, I steamed it, barbied it and it was really nice. So a glut of supply lead to a fall in price which created demand. I now have many more ways to cook, and meals I want to enjoy asparagus with. That new demand will be there next season, I wonder what the price will be?

All visibly competitive business reacts to supply and demand, the invisible hand. But in my opinion, this is only a very small part of our economy, which is one of the reasons I believe it doesn't work as well as it should.

# Four faces of the economy

We live in a relatively free society with relatively free markets which are sometimes competitive. That's a lot of caveats, but I think that it's important to understand where different business and government sectors operate, so that you can have a view on competition.

To me, there are four different provider types in the supply economy. All have a role on the demand side as well but I want to look at how much competition and therefore innovation, touches each of these sectors. The four sectors I identify are;

1. Government
2. Corporations
3. Regulated sector
4. visibly competitive businesses

## 1. Government

Governments supply a lot of services to the community. Policing, defence, NHS, pensions and prisons to name a few. Our government currently spends around 43% of the entire gross domestic product of the UK. How much competition is there when you deal with the government? I struggle to think of an occasion when I have had a free, visible choice of services that they provide. Bins emptied on a Tuesday – 'any chance of coming back on Friday?' - don't make me laugh. When you may be offered a choice, say of which GP to go to, this is a non-visible choice as you have no real way to compare their service. We are just looking for a decent, sympathetic doctor with warm hands.

Government has no tomato effect. Government services are policy lead, not consumer lead. You get what you are given and any minor innovation is slow and often, sad to say, misguided.

## 2. Corporations

We can define corporations as being businesses with a scale and reach to be involved in many areas of business and with a heavy influence on their market sector. How do you get on with corporations? I think it's safe to say that some are more competitive and innovative than governments, after all most of them (privatised utilities excluded) get to their size through the normal competitive process.

However 'The Corporates' is often used as a term of abuse now because they use their size and influence, through lobbying, to corrupt government at all levels. Public Finance Initiative, sweetheart tax deals, tax haven usage and 'bid to fail' deals all show the worst of many corporates today.

Virgin trains called foul when they weren't awarded the east coast mainline contract a few years ago. The bid had cost them £15M. Consider that, just placing a bid for the contract costs £15 million. This limits this type of business opportunity to the chosen few who have the financial clout to make such a bid.

Many companies also bid to fail, a competitive bid is placed but some time into the contract they say, we're running behind, you've changed your mind or other problems. The corporates then demand more money to fix the problems and to avoid public disquiet, the government normally coughs up and defends the contractor. This is 'bid to fail' and it makes billions for many government contractors especially in defence and computer contracts like the abandoned national NHS database and national fire service systems. Billions!

The tax office love to give our money away. They have made countless 'sweetheart' deals with banks and corporates. In one such deal Microsoft was let off around £100m. Vodafone, Goldman Sachs and many more. Billions!

The banks, bailout, no senior figures in prison, business as usual. Billions!

Public Finance Initiative contracts where we pay up to seven times the cost of the school or hospital buildings back to the corporate finance companies. The maintenance contracts allow firms to charge outrageous sums for changing a light bulb or repairing a door. Billions!

Serco and G4S were found to be charging for tagging dead or non-existent prisoners in order to overcharge on a government contract. No one from these companies has joined the prison ranks as they are essentially protected. It would look bad on a minister's judgement to send their preferred contractor to jail. If I had stolen millions from the government? If you had? What do you reckon would happen?

These advantages entrench the corporates, delay or remove innovation from services, transfer huge sums to them from us with limited accountability, while all the time enjoying government protection.

It used to be a mystery to me why there were so many 'anti capitalist' demonstrations over the last twenty years. Didn't capitalism win? It gave us all these benefits (tomatoes and wetsuits etc), so what's the beef? Now I'm beginning to understand where the problems lie. With the banks benefitting from all that bailout money which will end up costing us all, I might be ready for the barricades myself.

## 3. The Regulated sector

This will include lawyers, dentists, health and safety officers, accountants, surgeons, doctors, architects and other professions and functions that are regulated by a law or professional body. This sector is characterised by mostly non-visible competition. All these professions are in competition with their peers and some have advertising campaigns directed at the public like architects or dentists. But the difference here is that it's almost impossible to judge the quality of the service of these providers as they are services; you can only judge the book by the cover. You can of course, after the event, judge outcomes but even then it is often difficult to compare. Do you read all the legal documents a solicitor provides and after getting one lot of documents, do you go and get some different ones to compare? Not at these prices ehh!

Almost no-one chooses to spend money on health and safety or PAT testing or any other legal requirements laid upon us. We find a provider, we pay.

The regulated sector is notionally but not visibly competitive and innovation tends to be industry lead rather than consumer lead. The regulated sector nearly always has the most expensive labour rates out there as well. This makes it a special case in the economy and thus leaves us with just one truly competitive sector.

## 4. Visibly competitive businesses.

You name it, pubs, clubs, hairdressers, tool manufacturers, builders merchants, jet engine manufacturers, shops.

I have never bought a jet engine, and yes I know it's usual to lease engine hours now rather than buying one but indulge me. If you need to buy something as complex as a jet engine, the process is a visibly competitive one. You compare the upfront cost, running cost, life cycle, pollution and maintenance regimes for engines of the available manufacturers, Rolls Royce, GE, Pratt and Whitney etc. You choose an engine.

The most competitive businesses to be in are ones with zero cost of entry and zero barriers to exit. This is where the modern tomato came from. If you go to a restaurant and are not greatly impressed by their food or service, you may never go back. It doesn't cost you anything to remove your business, you don't have to work out a contract or credit. You just don't go again. In this type of business, innovation is nearly always consumer lead so amazingly, we tend to get what we want. This is the bit the other three business types don't generally have. That is why this is the most competitive, innovative and dynamic business type. It's a shame then that it is so overlooked by the banking sector as I will explain later.

# Capitalism

Capitalism should be about the actions of the market directing capital (profits) to successful businesses. For the businesses it is about the profit motive. For the customer it's about buying the best products and services on a cost versus benefits basis.

The visibly competitive portion of any economy is the where the exercise of capitalism is at it's most immediate. The market system coupled with businesses using efficient working practices provide profits that can then be re-invested. It's this mechanism that is at the heart of capitalism. It's my opinion that we don't have much of a capitalist system left in the UK.

Adam Smith, the legendary economist, warned that the market would tend towards the development of cartels and monopolies, and therefore some regulation would be needed to prevent this negative effect.

I believe Adam Smith would be deeply unimpressed with our current version of capitalism. Big corporates, privatised utilities, big brands and media are all tending towards cartel and monopolistic practices that are only tenuously competitive. Our regulation is almost completely useless at protecting the consumer and smaller competing businesses from these practices.

When people complain about capitalism itself, they are usually commenting on the state of our particular version of this system without considering its legitimacy. Capitalism can have many forms but it is, I believe, the only system that can be adapted to create wealth.

Individuals often don't see themselves as capitalists. But the truth is, whenever you spend money within the corporate, regulated or visibly competitive businesses, you are a part of the capitalist system. Choosing a big mac over pub lunch, directs capital (profits) to a large American corporation rather than a local family or business for instance.

All spending choices are capitalist! It's the lack of meaningful choices that reduces the power of capitalism and brings calls for more state intervention. But to me, the notion that a government employee will tell you where to eat your lunch is as stupid as expecting other government employees to decide on how a train service is run or where to build a hospital. Capitalism, in it's truer forms directs profits to businesses that deliver the goods and services people choose, so without a proper choice, capitalism won't work and a system without choice cannot be called capitalist.

**Video 5. 6mins -**

Youtube search - How to improve capitalism.
https://youtu.be/YOaJe68C-bU?list=PLD7u4sAYcu8qZc2JbDTX_cc28siMUoNOo

# Privatisation

Let's face it, privatisation has had a pretty chequered history and as a result, has very negative connotations amongst the general public. Not unfairly I would say. The utilities, railways, prisons and many other privatised services have had their privatised status badly structured. Privatising without competition doesn't work. Southern Rail for instance would be out of business for sure if you could climb on a competitors train and actually get to work on time. Because of the type of privatisation that has been imposed, we have far worse service, at a much higher cost than we should have, in many of the services we consume.

The terrible performance of the regulators in these industries is also partly to blame for their poor performance, lack of investment and cartel like lack of competition. I believe privatisation needs to be rehabilitated so that we can privatise for the benefit of consumers first.

The model for most government privatisations has been to find a single provider for a service via a bidding process that can cost bidders millions. This restricts not only the list of bidders but also the subsequent competition and innovation as the winning bidder has a contract for a number of years over which time they need to make profits, not improve services. The companies bidding for contracts also have to cover the massive cost of all bids they make from the few bids they win.

The winning bidders are sometimes overseen by the regulators such as OfGen (rubbish) OfWat (pretty rubbish) Ofcom (rubbish) OfSted (mostly rubbish), in fact I think all the regulators are not a patch on competition as a mechanism for ensuring good performance.

A more successful model of privatisation which could be a more beneficial way of organising government spending would be the 2012 Olympic Delivery Authority.

As a single QuANGO (Quasi Autonomous Non Governmental Organisation - translated means - Government Organisation) looking after a complex project they were able to organise in a way that made use of many businesses both large and small. This allowed companies not normally able to bid into this process as they didn't bid to build an entire stadium but specific parts of each project. Although far from a total success, they did bring the project in under their budget, this I believe, would be a better way to deploy government funds on the infrastructure programs we need in the future.

The privatisation of existing services, including the NHS is a far more emotive subject, but one that needs to be tackled. The biggest problem with the NHS is the basic design, not the funding. We have gone for massive hospitals catering for everything, all under one roof. They operate as a state monopoly and act like it. The monopoly removes choice from the recipient of service but can also remove our responsibilities for our health as well as we don't pay.

You often hear the case that we can't trust private firms to look after our health. This seems rather odd, we trust them to look after our food, surely nothing is more important than food in terms of our health. (You can make a good case for water but bear with me please). Just consider how wonderful our supermarkets are, we have bigun's and now the 'Express' style market is growing. Convenient, local, mostly cheap, All because of competition, the 'invisible hand' guided the market to deliver what we want. Supermarkets work on super tight margins and if a structure was put into place that delivered real competition rather than government favour, we could have the same revolution in health as we have in food.

In the long run we need to bring all government projects down to a size where competition can drive innovation and we will need to accept that private companies will make profits from public money (it's not as if they don't now, they just get it without the competition and customer satisfaction). Competition and sensible regulation will have the effect of controlling these profits whereas the monopoly status of many current governmental services guarantees waste, corruption and inefficiency.

# Money

What exactly is money? Without understanding money as a concept as well as a function of our economy, you cannot understand economics.

The normal definition of money requires it to do three things. It needs to be a unit of account, a medium of exchange and a store of value.

Unit of account: Money needs to be units that everyone agrees are of equal monetary value, a pound stirling, an ounce of gold, a Nectar point. These individual units often need to be divisible into smaller units to allow accurate pricing without being cumbersome to use and compute.

A medium of exchange: Money should allow a holder to exchange that currency for a product, service or other currency at an agreed rate. 1 ounce of gold = $1354.20, £1.20 for a loaf of bread, a haircut costs £8.50.

A store of value: Tricky, but ignoring *inflation* for now, if you hold pounds sterling for a couple of years you will still be able to buy the haircut or loaf of bread. Gold's a commodity whose price can vary, but you can exchange your pounds for the current exchange price.

Money is also primarily a convention. Money is money because we all agree it's money. This is a lot more fragile than we think. We have had decades of relative economic success and stability, so we in the UK just accept that the pound is money, end of.

Money is a convention but sometimes the dominant currency becomes devalued. The most damaging devaluation is the loss of trust, this can bring any currency down. We are used to the pound and for the time being it works and it's fairly well trusted. It's our money, it's our convention. In other parts of the world though there are different conventions on what constitutes money or currency.

In Kenya for instance, you can spend Kenyan shillings, you can easily spend euros and sometimes British pounds and US dollars. You can also use a credit card (debt as money) and among Kenyans living away from normal banking facilities, mobile air time is a very popular currency. I think this is a fascinating, organic development of flexible money systems and a challenge to our more rigid view of money.

We do use other forms of money, things like Nectar points, Air Miles and *crypto currencies* for example, are types of money, they are just a little more limited as a means of exchange and the store of value relies on *trusted third parties* who we don't know.

## Before money

Before we relied on money, early trade was done via the barter system. I give you a chicken, you give me two bags of wheat for instance. In early agrarian society people were mostly self sufficient as trade without money was very difficult. If you had excess chickens and needed wheat, you had to find someone with excess wheat who wanted a chicken. This is not a very flexible model for commerce, which is one of the reasons why there wasn't much trade done.

The other problems of barter is that there is a constantly fluctuating value for the items to be exchanged, is it a healthy big chicken or a scrawny thing with little meat? A chicken is not a set value. Wheat, properly handled, may be a bit easier to see as money. If a region were to fill a store with all the wheat produced and it was uniformly mixed, the quality problem would no longer be an issue as it would be uniform. The store would need to be designed to be secure, and to keep the wheat in top condition. The market could then value the quality of the chicken or any other commodity or service, by the amount of wheat someone was willing to give for it with no regard for the quality of wheat as this would be known to the market.

For money to exist and be efficient we need a money system that is representative of stored value, like the wheat.

## Classical Money.

All sorts of thing have been used as money in the past, shells, stones, clay tablets and metals. Gold is the most recognised form of money, digging it up and exchanging it for goods and services came about as there is a rarity and beauty in gold that people valued. This perceived value would eventually lead to the paper money we have today.

All though gold is money judged by the 3 rule definition, it didn't prove very easy to use. Carrying it was a bit of a bugger as someone had to have a set of scales on hand to check the value by weight. (Watch the classic '70s musical 'Paint your Wagon' for some of the problems).

The quality and purity of the metal was also open to question and possible fraud, but these issues were worked out.

As the amount of gold in the system increased, goldsmiths and banks opened to store the gold reserves of individuals and institutions. The banks would record the amounts of gold deposited in each account

The next important innovation was to divide the total in the ledger into units of an agreed value and issue pieces of paper that represented a known quantity of that reserve. These units would add up to the total deposit. A divisible unit of weight could be a pound of gold, hence the pound as a currency. (although, strictly speaking this originally referred to a pound weight of sterling silver, not gold)

So individual banks began printing their own notes for their customers who could exchange them for goods and services. Over time the bearer of the note stopped going to fetch the gold it represented from the bank and just relied on the note as it was a more convenient means of exchange. The holder of the note was confident that he had the store of value implied by the physical gold in a bank vault.

This form of currency is known as 'Gold Standard' where the amount of money in circulation is a representation of the amount of gold held within the banking system.

As I mentioned above, wheat could have been a store of value that became represented by paper, later gold became the store of value the paper represented. Oil could function in the same way, cigarettes in a prison could be represented by paper receipts and form a store of value. The way money came into existence was as a receipt for stored physical value.

This is an important concept that we mostly don't understand or question. Money is the physical thing, money is wheat, gold, oil or cigarettes, the paper receipts we use are the 'currency'. If you are a farmer with a chicken being offered a receipt for some wheat held in the store, but you knew the store was empty, (ie no wheat), you wouldn't accept the receipt in exchange for your goods or services would you? You would demand physical wheat be given to you or no chicken!

And yet, now our currency represents almost nothing. The Bank of England has hardly any money (a physical thing as a store of value). There are around 310 tonnes of gold in the vaults, with total value today around £10 billion. Less than 0.1% of the currency in circulation in all forms and not enough to pay foreign holders of pounds. That would leave us with nothing.

Our currency isn't money, there is no money. Nothing. This is, I suspect, not how you imagined our money and hopefully this will make you a little concerned.

**Video 6, 30mins - Please watch Mike's videos.**

Youtube search - Secrets of Money Episode 1- Mike Maloney.
https://youtu.be/DyV0OfU3-FU

# Gold and Silver

Gold and silver are known as monetary metals as they have been used as a basis for, and an ingredient in money for centuries.

Central banks are keen that they should be seen as a bit of a relic and of no particular value other than as a commodity. And yet, behind the scenes there is a lot of official activity and this can be seen in the gold market especially. This activity involves gold price manipulation and certain central banks stacking their vaults high with the stuff.

The London Metals Exchange (LME) is the largest metals exchange in the world with a notional value of around £12 trillion a year. The world's total, above ground stock of gold (ie mined and refined) is thought to be only £7 trillion. So why the discrepancy? The word 'notional' value is very important in this context and this is where the manipulation exists.

To trade on the LME you don't necessarily need any gold, you just need to promise to supply it, at some point in the future, at a given price. This is known as a futures contract. The result of this, and other manipulations is that the amount of gold visible to the market is much bigger than the actual supply. This artificially expanded market size has the effect of suppressing the price.

Another form of market expansion is the use of Exchange Traded Fund (ETF) gold. Although the ETF's refer to physical gold, and they should have some vaulted gold to back them, this is on a fractional basis, ie they only hold a fraction of the total ETF value. Again this has the effect of artificially expanding the visible supply. The expanded notional supply of gold holds the price down.

Other forms of precious metals skulduggery involve gold swaps and leasings from the central banks. Sovereign gold repatriations and acquisition. China and Russia for instance are in the process of building large stocks of gold while the price remains artificially suppressed.

There are a large group of gold investors, known as 'gold bugs' who believe that this manipulation is not sustainable and at some point, the market will discover the true quantity and therefore value of gold, which they hope is in the tens of thousands per ounce rather than £1,300 as it is today.

Silver is less manipulated than gold as there is an industrial component to this market. Silver is extremely widely used by industry, especially as a conductor in electronics but this is used in very small amounts, usually plated onto base metals. This means that although the total above ground stock is massive, most has been used and in a way that makes it uneconomical to recover. Silver is far more volatile in price, but because so much has been used and is essentially unrecoverable, the tradeable supply is far more scarce as well, so this is also an option for a currency hedge or long term saving.

If you are interested in holding gold or silver, I would buy the physical metal and hold it yourself, possibly buried in the garden or you can have it vaulted. Only the physical bars are a relatively sure investment. I suspect the ETF's will be one of the first victims of the next big financial bubble. (Look into the Minsky moment for more).

**Video 7, 30mins**
Youtube search - Death of dollar reserve status - Secrets of money Ep 3.
https://youtu.be/y-IemeM-Ado?list=PLE88E9ICdipidHkTehs1VbFzgwrq1jkUJ

**Video 8. 1hr 30mins**
Youtube search - The Case for $20,000 oz Gold - Debt Collapse.
https://youtu.be/tj2s6vzErqY

# More Money History

The next major change in our money system was the emergence of the central banks as the sole source of new money currency.

During the early gold standard period the fractional lending system developed. 'Fractional' means that the banks only had a 'fraction' of the gold they would need to cover all redemptions.

Private banks noticed that people came to claim their physical gold (redemptions) less and less as trust in the banks and the paper they issued increased. The bankers saw this as an opportunity to create some new money. They could after all, just print some more of their own notes and, as long as there were low levels of redemptions, no one would know.

UK private banks started the printing presses. This caused massive inflation in the mid 1800's and in 1844, the then prime minister, Robert Peel, instigated the 'banking reform act' which made it illegal for any bank, other than the Bank of England, to print money currency. In this way, the government could control the money supply and the country would have a uniform currency and rates of interest would also be controlled.

The problem with the 'banking reform act' was that it didn't foresee balance sheet lending. Although the act prevented individual banks from 'creating' new currency money with a printing press, it didn't specifically prevent them from putting numbers on a ledger that represented money. After all, when you buy an item like a car or a house through a bank loan, or even a coffee with a debit/credit card, you don't see any money as currency. It's all done on a ledger and this is why banks still have the power to create money. This is something I imagine Robert Peel had not intended to happen but the consequences are clear.

While the Bank of England operated a gold standard, where the currency they printed was a receipt for stored physical gold things were mostly OK and our economy had very strong growth in the late 1800's.

Governments of this period spent only a small fraction of what they do now. We had no welfare state or other expensive projects to fund, so taxes and spending were low.

Wars are usually the main instigator of major financial crises and these crises often instigate revolutions, coups and changes in political power. A good case in point is Germany

Adolf Hitler came to power after the Weimar republic caused massive inflation as they tried to deal with poverty caused by war reparations required after the first world war. He came to power on a promise of rebuilding the German state. He also had plans to dominate Europe.

The second world war saw Great Britain stand alone against the Germans who had occupied most of continental Europe with a modern war machine built up after Adolf Hitler took power in 1933. The British had left it a bit late to prepare their armed forces as we still had a lot of soldiers on horseback and aeroplanes with more than one wing up front. We needed to re arm but we were struggling after a disastrous revaluation of gold after the first world war had broken our economy (blame the then Chancellor of the Exchequer Winston Churchill for that one I'm afraid). The upshot was we went rather 'cap in hand' to uncle Sam for help with the war effort, as we set all available production to new armaments. Uncle Sam was happy to help us but wanted payment in gold for any help under the premise that they were staunchly neutral so this was strictly a business deal. These payments finished the emptying of the British vaults that had started during the first world war (USA late again). American and European banks and corporations also made huge sums supplying the Nazi government before and during the war. This too was a surprise when I discovered it. For instance, the Luftwaffe could have been grounded at any time if the American company Standard Oil (Esso today), had stopped supplying them with tetraethyl lead, an additive required for their fuel.

http://reformed-theology.org/html/books/wall_street/chapter_04.htm

That all meant that by the end of the war, America, not us, was the richest country in the world.

After the second world war there was a meeting at 'Bretton Woods' in New Hampshire state that set out the structure of the post war economic framework. The dollar would be the dominant currency which would be gold fixed. This meant that it wasn't an equivalent value of gold to dollars, as this would have been too few dollars to support world trade, so there were only $60 worth of gold for every $100 currency.

All other free floating currencies would be pegged to the dollar and thus to gold. Only central banks could redeem their dollars for gold in this system and all was fine until the Vietnam war. America's growing war debts made the French, as well as others, very nervous about the prospect of countries redeeming their dollars for the gold in the USA's vaults, leaving them holding just paper. Eventually Charles De Gaulle sent his gun boats to New York to pick up their gold and seeing this, realising the trouble they were in, President Nixon decided to take America off the gold fix standard in 1971. We haven't seen a gold backed currency system since.

Americans had got used to having the world's dominant currency and the demand for dollars, and dollar debt this created. America wanted – indeed needed this to continue. The US dollar being the global reserve currency allowed the US government to spend, spend, spend on welfare and war with printed, not earned money.

Nixon sent Henry Kissinger to make an alliance with the Saudi's to ensure all their oil traded was paid for in dollars. This meant that any country wanting to buy oil from Saudi Arabia had to first exchange their own currency for dollars before paying for the oil. In return for this arrangement, America lent military and diplomatic support for Saudi Arabia's regional dominance and guaranteed protection from their neighbours and especially Israel. This 'petro dollar' standard was introduced after considerable diplomatic posturing, but by 1975 it had been introduced to all OPEC countries who also feared Israel's military power (aided by America). The new petro dollar system allowed the US to print as much money as it liked; it was a master stroke. Not only did the OPEC countries insist on payment in dollars for their oil, they also bought huge amounts of US debt (Treasury *bonds*) with their profits. What a bonanza for the US treasury!

As demand for oil increased, more and more dollars could be printed and more US debt found willing buyers. America's foreign policy should also be seen as an attempt to maintain just the right level of tension in the middle east to ensure this system continues, as well as America's motive to protect this system by war.

America made good on their promises in 1991. In the first Gulf war. Iraq had invaded Kuwait and threatened regional stability, America restored the status quo, but later came to regret not removing Saddam Hussain as leader of Iraq at that time.

Saddam was no friend of the American's and the second gulf war in 2003 was partly a reaction to Iraq starting to sell oil in other currencies, unilaterally threatening the petrodollar. It also didn't help that Saddam had signed large oil deals with America's rivals, Russia and China as well as France. You may remember that it was principally these three countries that opposed the invasion dreamt up by the US under the 'dodgy dossier' sham of weapons of mass destruction. This is the main reason the USA were so keen to invade a country that had no WMDs, were also not implicated at all by 9/11 and the subsequent 'war on terror'. The day after Iraq's inevitable defeat, oil trading went back to dollars and America took control of their oil supplies.

The other consequence of the petrodollar system was that all countries who needed oil, also now needed dollars. The foreign exchange markets are an expensive way to get dollars. If you keep selling your own currency into the market for dollars, it's value drops relative to the dollar and then your next purchase of oil is more expensive and so on. This gave a massive incentive to developing countries like Japan and then China to become exporters, especially to America, so they could be paid in dollars which they could then use for purchasing the oil they needed. The dollars then go back to the USA via treasury bond purchases by the oil producing states, another winner.

When you consider oil as money, this makes some sense as it's a valuable, finite resource that is hard to dig up, just like gold. It doesn't look as good on our fingers though. There are now many moves against the petrodollar system and it may not be long before there are enough non-dollar players to tip the market. This will be a disaster for the USA, one they may struggle to survive and could lead to a seismic shift in world power away from Washington towards China.

**Video 9. 30mins**

Youtube search -Seven stages of empire- Hidden Secrets Of Money Ep 2 - Mike Maloney

https://youtu.be/EdSq5H7awi8?list=PLE88E9ICdipidHkTehs1V bFzgwrq1jkUJ

**Video 10. 30mins**

Youtube search - Rise of Hitler was ECONOMICS - Secrets of money Ep5 - Mike Maloney

https://youtu.be/OQWMd_NPSBA?list=PLE88E9ICdipidHkTe hs1VbFzgwrq1jkUJ

# Lending

'1984' by George Orwell, if you have not read it, I would highly recommend doing so. If you have read it, isn't it time to read it again, It's the most up to date book, prescient, brilliant.

Lending is classic Orwellian double speak.

Banks do not lend money. Seriously. Private banks don't lend money. **They create it**. Lending is double speak.

Let's use some words. If I lend you my lawnmower for the day and you return it in the same condition, we are friends. That's a loan.

If I lend you my lawnmower for a month and you return it with no petrol and the blade is blunt, we are friends but I ask you to pay for the petrol and the sharpening of the blades. Still a loan? Maybe, just.

I'm a rental company and you have my lawnmower for a month, you get charged for a proportion of the capital cost of the mower, service, fuel and a profit margin. This is rent.

This is the thing to understand, banks don't even have to deal with the capital cost. Banks don't pass money from a saver to a borrower, they create it. When a bank makes a loan they create the money out of nothing by double entry bookkeeping. Banks are granted this massive privilege, just by entering numbers into a ledger, now a computer, they are allowed to create new money almost without limit.

The banking reform act of 1844 prevented private banks from printing their own money currency, but it didn't prevent them from creating money on a balance sheet.

When it comes to borrowing from the banks, we see this new money as digits on a page. The bank has created an asset on their accounts and a liability on yours. This double entry book keeping is like Newton's third law, 'every action has an equal and opposite reaction', a debit and a credit, an asset and a liability.

This is sometimes a little difficult to understand but when a borrower needs money, a banks creates the money by making you liable (credit) to repay the sum you need. The word credit comes from the latin word for belief. i.e, we, the bank, believe you will pay us back. It's this contract between a borrower and the bank that brings the new money into existence.

You can create money this way in your local pub. If you have the cost of your drinks put on a tab, you have created credit. Your landlord 'believes' you will pay but no money has actually changed hands for the goods you have consumed. You still have the money in your pocket and you will pay for the bill 'in the future'.

In a bank, loans are shown as an asset (debit or debt to be paid) on the banks balance sheet. So as the value of loans go up, the banks asset value goes up as well.

The confusion here is that when we see our bank statement is in credit, we associate this with having money. To understand this paradox you need to remember that the bank writes the statements from their perspective, i.e. if the bank is holding your money it's a liability to them. A liability to them is a credit.

This balance sheet process has the effect of creating money currency out of nothing. New 'money' is created by the banks and becomes part of the money supply, 97% of which is debt. The remaining three percent is our cash money, paper and coins.

Do banks *lend*? I would say no. Banks don't 'lend' money, they rent you a privilege, the privilege of money creation. They have nothing to lend, they create a facility out of nothing and charge you rent. The 'interest' we all pay is rent paid to private banks for adding numbers to a computer. Billions of pounds a year goes on this rent, but no one is in a hurry to explain this truth, least of all, the banks.

# Savers

When we save money within the banking system we are further facilitating their lending. The money we deposit into a bank, that isn't used to cancel a debt, is effectively given to the bank for them to use as they see fit. The 'money' isn't held in storage as such, it's just numbers on a page of accounts. The deposit can, and usually is used by the bank to expand their capital reserves so they can lend out more money. They can do this without conscience as the government guarantees all deposits within the bank up to £85,000 per person, per bank. This is a gross distortion of business practice and a 'moral hazard' for the banks (assuming they have any morals).

Saving outside the banking system will be more likely to secure your deposit as money, or as a thing like a premium bond or a share for instance. Another way to save is to buy a thing with value and hold onto it. Things like gold or silver coins, collectables and art, anything with a commodity value that is likely to have a long term tradeable value.

One of the tragic effects of money creation and saving is that people who are already quite rich, homeowners who have high equity value like the baby boomers for instance, are usually saving to buy stuff. When I save money it might be for a new computer or big telly, these things are not going up in price so the fact that I'm not getting a return on my savings doesn't really hurt me. Younger people however may want to save to get a down payment on a house. They are the big losers as the money creation policies of the last three governments (and last two Bank of England governors) have created massive asset price inflation so they save devalued money and fall further and further behind house prices. Interest on savings is 1%, house price inflation is around 7%. Only a crash or taxes to favour the young can end that disparity.

# Interest

The interest charged by the banks isn't in the system, as only the principal amount is created.

This means that the interest has to be created as someone else's debt, transferred to a debtor via normal GDP activities and then go back to the banks. This creates a system which always needs more and more debt money to pay the interest on the previous debt money, it's endless but, I suspect, unsustainable.

For instance, if you borrow £10,000 to buy a car and the effect of the interest and fees is that you will end up paying £11,350 for that car. The extra £1,350 hasn't been created by the bank as it was only the principal amount that was entered in the computer at the time you took out the loan. The £1,350 has to be taken from someone else, normally by working it off in employment or selling an asset. The £1,350 work you do, for the bank, is their rent on the loan, the rent on the privilege of money creation.

If you don't repay the £10,000 plus interest, the bank has not 'lost' this money because it was nothing more than numbers on a balance sheet. All they have lost is the potential income on the rent of their privilege, a reduction of their asset value and possibly a small decrease in their capital reserves. The idea that banks lose money because of bad debt is not strictly true (if the debt is issued in our own currency).

Interest is a very blunt tool and creates poverty and debt slavery for most. The Islamic faith outlaws the charging of interest for this reason and this is also why Jewish money lenders were so despised for centuries, they charged interest.

The old testament contains accounts of the concept of 'debt jubilee' where every 50 years, debts were cancelled to allow people to escape their debt slavery. There is a current campaign for the same now. www.jubileedebt. org.uk

The fact that we have been on near zero interest rates for a decade has allowed an expansion of the money supply via bank lending that will be very hard to unwind without a major event like a crash in sterling and subsequent recession. Because of the ever increasing *debt burden,* interest rates will not go back to historical norms until there has been a big reset of the money system. Near-zero interest rates are the new norm as any significant increase would create recession for the economy and a collapse of spending both public and private.

The rate of interest is variable, massively variable. The very rich, like countries or large corporations only pay a very small rate, UK debt is trading around 1.3%, so is Greece, funnily enough. Coca Cola or Ford will pay 2-4% on their bonds. We pay 3-4% on mortgages at the moment, but in the consumer credit world, the rates really start to ramp up. Overdrafts 6-20%, credit cards 20-50% and the grandaddy of them all, payday lenders 100-1500%. I know this is true, it's advertised on the telly.

Have you noticed that they have stopped saying "One thousand, two hundred and eighty four percent representative APR". Very old hat, they now say "One, two, eight, four representative APR". It sounds so much cheaper without mentioning the 'thousand' word doesn't it?

The poor of our countries are paying huge amounts to the banks and money lenders for the same facility that some countries get for free. Is the risk of Greece defaulting on their debt really reflected in the price? Are the risks of lending to someone needing a payday loan reasonably reflected in the price? I'm afraid I don't believe it is. The way interest is charged is a drain on resources, especially for the poorer people in society, to enrich the banks and their associates.

Interest rates are set by the banks as part of monetary policy. Interest rates are low at the moment to ease the debt burden. The rates will remain low as long as we see little inflation as expressed by the Consume Price Index (CPI).

During a time of increased *inflation* however, governments tend to raise interest rates to discourage extra borrowing and this has the added effect of extracting money from the economy via increased debt servicing costs. As the amount of money in the economy is reduced, this will also reduce growth or create a recession. This means balancing interest rates and economic cycles is very difficult to achieve.

# Debt Cycles

Debt causes cycles that are both short and long term and also at a macro and micro economic scale. Debt is a process where you borrow your future earnings. So if you earn £20,000 a year but need some more to cover life's expenses, you can borrow. If you borrow £5000 for instance, your effective earnings (net income) for that year are £25,000, but in subsequent years your net income could be less than £20,000 as you pay this money back. This causes an up swing and then down turn in your income. That is a short term debt cycle. The way to avoid the downturn is to increase your earnings through more hours or a better rate of pay, or to spend the £5000 on something that will create an income for you.

Most countries are also in debt cycles as well and in the same way they can avoid or mitigate the downturn if they spend the money borrowed on productive investment. A country can also get more income by working harder, being more productive or seeing an increase in the working population and increasing their GDP.

Long term debt cycles are a little different. A long term debt cycle often ends badly if unchecked and will require a restructuring of the financial system. On an individual level this means a person might take on more and more debt to cover interest and avoid the worst of the downswings of the short term debt cycle. Eventually, if this isn't remedied, the underlying debt will build to a stage where bankruptcy beckons. Bankruptcy will change the debt situation but also the lifestyle and assets of the bankrupt individual.

Countries can also go through debt cycles due to the same problems and with the same results. Even big countries do this. The USA had a major deleveraging in the 1929 crash which wrote off masses of debt, ruined millions of people and left a very weak financial system and it took a nationwide gold confiscation and a war to revive this fully.

The UK has a had a couple of major deleveraging events recently, one was after the second world war when GDP shrank drastically as we stopped building tanks and the welfare state started boosting overall government spending.

The chart below shows private debt increasing rapidly since the bank deregulation in the early 1980's. You can see by the rate of increases in private debt, that we are now locked into a different situation than before with rate of indebtedness at much, much higher levels. I have already outlined how the debt burden forces us into an ever increasing level of debt, so even though the debt has come down some after the 2007/8 crisis, it is unlikely that this will prevent the previous high from being overtaken in the next few of years.

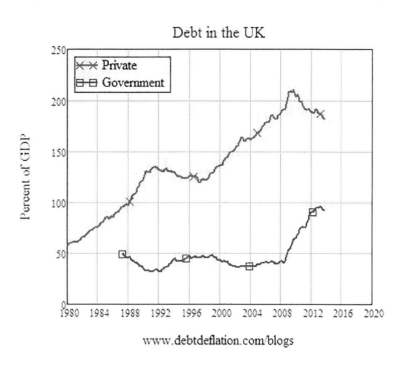

### Debt in the UK

www.debtdeflation.com/blogs

With kind permission of Professor Steve Keen from the Debt Deflation blog and author of 'Debunking Economics' and 'Can We Avoid Another Financial Crisis'

The massive rise in private debt along with the increasing debts of the government means that without a significant improvement in the balance of payments and productivity, we will have to keep borrowing more and more money. The only real question is who will take on this future debt, government or the private and business sectors.

**Video 11 - 30 minutes**

Youtube search - How The Economic Machine Works by Ray Dalio
https://youtu.be/PHe0bXAIuk0?list=PLD7u4sAYcu8qZc2JbDTX_
cc28siMUoNOo

# The Debt Burden

The debt burden is how we describe the aggregated effect of the interest payment required to service debts, as well as the capital in relation to our income (salary or GDP for instance). Generally government debt is the main focus, but nowadays private debt far exceeds government debt so we should consider both.

The mortgage market dominates private lending in the UK and therefore acts as an anchor on the rate of interest on all debt. If we bundle all loans of all types together the average rate, held down by mortgages and government debt (almost free at the moment), would probably be around 3-4%. This is a guess on my part and just to illustrate the problem, so let's take a relatively low number of 3% per annum.

In that case, the money supply has to increase by 3% next year, just to pay the interest on last years money supply. New debt needs to be issued at this rate or faster, or the total money supply will fall due to interest payments pulling money out of circulation. This reduction in money supply could have the effect of creating a recession. To avoid a recession, we need to borrow more money to pay off our previous debts and so on. This is very much the situation we are in today.

This is not completely or solely true of course. A reduction in the debt burden can be accounted for in other ways. Primarily through improving demographics, productivity and producing a trade surplus. In the UK for the last 20 years we have really struggled with the latter two areas. Increased immigration and an upturn in birth rate recently could help the demographic situation but we haven't seen a real increase in productivity for two decades. Therefore increasing public and private debt is the quickest and easiest, although ultimately futile solution to our debt burden.

Our debt burden creates an ever-increasing demand for new money supply and our current system has been rigged to make sure this new money keeps flowing. Student loans and car financing are areas of credit growth that have been introduced in the last few years to facilitate higher indebtedness but anybody should be able to see that 'real' growth is very difficult to achieve whilst servicing a sizeable debt burden.

Improvements in demographics, productivity or balance of payments are possible but are more difficult to achieve and for politicians, these solutions are too slow to implement. We, the voters, don't like to be told we may have to wait for 20 plus years for an improvement in our living standards even though, this is what is happening to the middle and lower classes since the turn of the century.

Our accumulated debt will become a major problem both as individuals, families and for debt soaked countries.

## Demographics

Demographics is the practice of describing the distribution within a population by age, ethnicity, socio economic groupings, religion and any other differentiating factor. Demographics are a major concern for many western countries, especially age related factors. For strong growth to occur, absent a transformational technology shift, a country needs just the right balance of age groups within the population. A distribution that favours younger working age people with less dependants per person will give a strong workforce that should produce growth and increased production. Most western countries are tending towards the opposite situation where retirees outnumber the working population.

In the baby boom era (and I'm near the peak in '63), the UK nearly got the birthrate to three children per household and our economy has been boosted by their subsequent entry into the workforce. Since 1978 the UK has been at a much lower level of births which indicates a decline in the working population was due sometime around 2020-2030. The pragmatic solution was immigration and preferably, immigration from countries with a tradition of larger family sizes. The policy appears to have worked and was conducted at a speed that allowed good levels of integration. We now appear to have an improving trend towards larger families and although well below the peak, this means that our economy is more likely to avoid a major demographic shift. The ageing baby boomers are going to be heavy burden nonetheless.

Meanwhile, other countries who have let their demographic problem fester (like Germany and Japan) are in big trouble. The average age of a farmer in Japan is 66, and they now sell more adult nappies than infant sized. Germany panicked and let hundreds of thousands of refugees into their country, which in itself is a large demographic problem, not solution. The recent intake of refugees was predominantly young men and therefore could prove to be a destabalising force within Germany. China created a similar 'own goal' by introducing the one child per family rule which has created a male dominated, and declining workforce which will have a massive effect on their economy quite soon.

A government needs to manage the demographics of the country well if the economy is to survive.

**Video 12 - 25 mins**

Youtube search - 101 East - Ageing Japan
www.youtu.be/R8wdLWUEnzI

# Productivity

We have to go to work. While there, we may as well make as much money as we can. Productivity is simply a measure of how much stuff we produce per hour. Although we have seen some very small gains overall, they have been nowhere near the level required to service our debt burden.

I am self employed and run a small business. It's smaller now than when my father started it in 1979. But now it's far more productive through investment in CAD/CAM technology and time management than it has ever has been. As the owner, I was motivated to increase my productivity because I would benefit directly. The problem is, to an extent, that I was also motivated to reduce my costs by reducing staff levels.

Productivity improvement is absolutely crucial to overcoming the debt burden. Through investment in new technologies and working patterns enabled by mass communication tools, we should have seen a transformational increase in productivity in the last decade but it hasn't appeared. I suspect that the improvements in the portion of the economy where major gains can be made, mostly manufacturing, cannot be enough to overcome the drag created by government, corporates and the regulated sector.

One of the issues in a 'post industrial' society, one that has a heavy bias towards services, is that the productivity gains are harder to achieve as services are much harder to leverage with new technology and innovation. A hairdresser can't use two pairs of scissors at once on two heads, anyway this service is often about the experience and less about efficiency. Most services are trapped in this pervasive inefficiency. As I mentioned above, the services from regulated sector in particular are also very expensive.

Wages are very difficult to shift downwards, economists call this 'sticky'. Wages are stickier in the government and regulated sectors as they are more insulated from innovation and competition than the other sectors of the economy (Corporate and Visibly competitive).

Wages around the minimum levels have been stagnant in the UK for years meaning that labour is cheap. For productivity to improve, business has to invest in the skills of their personnel and the equipment, processes and input factors (like stock and subcontractors) that they rely on. This is much more likely to happen when labour is expensive.

# Balance of Payments

The balance of payments is largely associated with the trade balance of a country, the difference between the value of exports and imports. This trade balance then has international capital flows added to it to give the balance of payments.

The situation with the UK's balance of payments is probably the weakest aspect of our economy.

If you think of your own household finance, your balance of payments would be the difference between what you earn and what you spend. If it's positive, you should have some savings. If it's negative however, you will need to plug the gap with savings from a previous year, sell an asset or borrow the money. It's no different for countries.

The UK has a large trade deficit, a difference between what we import and export which we need to plug by selling assets or borrowing to avoid a current account deficit. (The current account is the total effect of balance of international payments, and domestic tax income, expenditure, savings, income and borrowing). In a household budget you would have the same factors that would make up the capital account.

Given that the UK has been running a balance of payments deficit in the last couple of decades, to help plug the gap we have tended to sell assets, such as large UK businesses, land and utilities to foreign investors and we are, thankfully, also very successful at attracting inward foreign investment (when a foreign company sets up a plant or office here - Nissan, Hitachi, Deutsche Bank). In recent years though, the UK has mostly relied on borrowing.

To relate this back to a household, as we earn less than we spend, to help balance the books we have to rent space in our family home to other people. Not a single lodger, but many people renting small spaces for storage for instance. Other people's stuff now fills one and a half bedrooms which we can no longer use. As this is still not enough to balance the books, we also borrow money from the neighbours. Luckily our family name is Cuthbert-Smyth from the noble lines of the Cuthberts and Smyths. The neighbours believe we're good for it. But how much can the Cuthbert-Smyths borrow from the neighbours before they get nervous?

The Cuthbert-Smyths have seven children of working age who all live in the remaining bedrooms and contribute to the family income. The neighbours seem to think they are all due for a promotion soon but what if one or two fall sick or lose their jobs?

This may seem a trivial analogy but this is an extremely simplified version of our current position. Enough creditors believe we are 'good for it', but coming to the end of a 30 year bond bull market, it may not be long before sentiment changes and we find ourselves in deep trouble.

America is far worse in real terms but they have (for now) the petro-dollar system keeping them going. The pound and our economy are not this fortunate.

Corporations and sovereign funds have bought up many businesses and assets within the UK which has the effect of exporting the talents and labour of many people working within our economy. We have sold and now export a large portion of our surplus which is paid to shareholders in Germany, Japan, Abu Dhabi, America and others. By selling these assets we have effectively reduced our ability to create wealth for our own benefit.

The balance of payments is a key indicator of the strength of a nation's economy and has an effect on the value of its currency. Foreign exchange traders (Forex) look to this and other indicators to set an exchange rate against other currencies. The German mark was a very strong currency during the later part of the 20th century. Germany's manufacturing industries created a very positive balance of payments and the mark's strength reflected this. In contrast, many other countries had a negative trade balance and therefore weaker currencies.

The advent of the euro was resisted by many in Germany who wanted to keep the mark, but Germany is by far the biggest winner from the euro system. Germany has increased its positive balance of payments relative to the rest of the euro zone and the rest of the world. Because the value of the euro is a reflection of the state of the eurozone as a whole, Germany's trading position is enhanced by a relatively cheap currency which promotes exports and their positive trade balance sucks currency out of the rest of the eurozone. With Germany having so much money saved, they are also the banker to the rest of the eurozone which gives them extreme power over the financial and therefore political direction of the EU.

There are two sides to every trade and the fact that the euro is relatively weak for Germany means it's relatively strong for nearly all the rest of the eurozone. Certainly all the southern states could do with a much cheaper currency but the euro system has no way of accommodating their relatively weak performance. The only tactic for them is internal deflation of wages and living standards. If they don't undergo internal deflation, their balance of payments will get much, much worse.

To go full circle, the southern states internal deflation, unemployment and general malaise maintains the euro weakness, better again for Germany. It's a crazy system but the politicians will not admit their failure.

Germany has a strong, positive balance of payments based on their trade. We do not.

Britain had a strong balance of payments surplus for a couple of centuries as we started the industrial revolution, colonised large parts of the world and used protectionist and exploitative trading policies. War, terror, sweat shops, slavery, child labour, excessive pollution and no sign of 'elf and safety. Britain has done it all and we got rich on it. We are now a little squeamish about other developing countries employing the same tactics we used but it's unrealistic to expect a country to go from relative poverty to prosperity without using at least some of these tactics. We, after all, had it easy as there were no countries with a more powerful position than Britain once the industrial revolution got going. It was a real and lasting revolution in production, trade and living standards for Britain's, eventually, not instantly.

All empires fade and the final straw was when our balance of payments went negative in the mid seventies and has, with a couple of brief exceptions, been in deficit ever since.

I believe that the financialisation of our post industrial economy has exacerbated this situation. The City of London does bring in a considerable amount of money into the country, but money is very liquid. If you deposit cash in an account in another country, it is relatively easy to withdraw it again unless the country in question puts in place 'capital controls' as happened in Greece and Cyprus recently. Capital controls will block the export of money from a country. London's position as a global financial centre makes a mass withdrawal seem unlikely but far from impossible. A future crisis in America or China could see huge sums being withdrawn from our financial markets almost instantly. We may have to introduce capital controls ourselves in this case to protect the value of the pound and prevent bank runs.

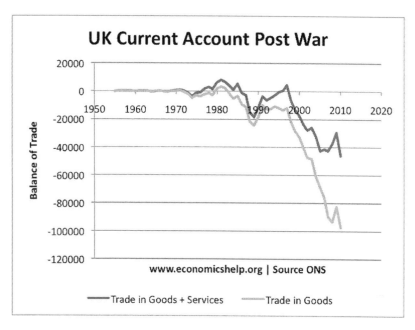

The buying and selling of equities doesn't greatly impact *GDP* but does create a large support service network. You can see by the chart above, our service sector is helping to alleviate the lack of physical exports. These services are things like finance, insurance, consultancy, architecture and education. Despite this our balance of payments is in a mess.

# The Paradox of the Debt Burden

What is most obvious way to deal with our debts? We have to pay them off don't we? What effect will this have on the economy though?

As we pay down debt, it has two major effects. As debt is paid down, as debt is money, money is destroyed and the total money supply reduces. Secondly, if we are paying down our debt, money that we could have been using to buy 'stuff' now goes back to the banks and doesn't become someone else's income, this will have the effect of reducing economic activity.

These two effects of paying down debt will reduce nominal GDP which will make it harder to keep paying down the debt. Economist call this 'a debt deflation spiral' or 'secular stagnation'.

Professor Steve Keen refers to this phenomenon, in a pithy reference to the 80's song as 'turning Japanese' as this debt deflation spiral is the trap the Japanese economy has been in for nearly thirty years. He really thinks so.

# Modern Money System

Our modern system is not gold based because this restricted the government from borrowing or creating new money in order to overpay for services and fighting wars. The system most people think we have now is referred to as 'fiat' money. The word 'fiat' means 'let it be so', in other words, the government says this is money now so just deal with it. Money, by decree.

This system relies on the ability of a government to tax the population to create the 'money value'.

I don't believe that we have a fiat money system in the UK, not really, not for a long time. This is so important, Gold or oil as money makes some sense but I have explained how those commodity backed systems worked and then failed. Fiat money sounds reasonable at first. A government has the power to raise taxes, to collect money from citizens to control the issued money and pay international debts.

Since the inception of the welfare state after the second world war, government spending has increased way ahead of GDP growth. Successive government's unwillingness to raise taxes and cut spending programmes has meant that governments have had to create more and more money to keep paying for the deficits that this produced

The real problem with our system is how new money is created. Money is created through the exchange of IOU's which will be covered in more detail later. The amount of money IOU's in the UK is vastly bigger than the ability of our government to tax the money back into a stable situation.

The money system in the UK is a debt based system. Debt is money. There is nothing behind the majority of our money, it depends on you and me and everyone else paying their mortgages, credit card bills and payday loans. Around 80% of all money and 97% of the money that touches the economy is debt. If we ever managed to pay it off, the economy would collapse. Our money is debt and our economy therefore is debt, which we as a country cannot be allowed to repay. If money is debt, and no one is in debt, there is no money.

Citizens must be in debt either personally or by proxy, through government or UK businesses.

If you and I pay off our debt, the government has to induce someone else to take on new debt to keep the show on the road. Students have recently become the best way of increasing the amount of debt money in the economy. This has nothing to do with funding education really, this is a distraction from the real reasons for student loans being introduced. Someone needed to be more in debt and after the last Labour government increased public expenditure so much, the political mood was for government debt to be reduced. After the 2010 election, the Conservative/Liberal coalition greatly increased the levels of student loans by raising the upper limit for tuition fees to £9k per annum (a threefold increase).

Latest estimates suggest students will leave university with an average of over £44,000 of debt each. Welcome to your role as money makers. There is no 'money' without debt. Debt is 'money'.

Have you seen the film 'The Matrix'. Our money system is like the matrix, we are all plugged into the system and it owns us. The reason our money system doesn't collapse today is that it's backed by a valuable commodity, our labour. If we continue to work and pay interest on our loans the matrix lives and thrives. Our labour is what allows all this to continue. It is clear to see how sensitive currency markets are to the labour numbers. If the employment rate goes down or productivity drops it means only one thing for a currency, devaluation. Conversely if employment goes up and productivity goes up, happy days. We no longer have gold to back our currency, we have us, the worker bees and our willingness to borrow.

This will seem very extreme to some people and it takes a bit of time to think about and understand. This is my opinion, but it's also a view being held by more and more people such as the 'occupy' group, 'Anonymous' and other protest movements are feeding on the disquiet people have of the financialisation of us!

Please watch 97% owned, it's a very well produced documentary and will give you more information on money and the effects it has on our lives. I have joined a campaign called Positive Money that is featured in this film.

## Video 13 - 2hrs 10 mins or a 54min version is available.

Search youtube - 97% Owned-Economic truth documentary
https://youtu.be/XcGh1Dex4Yo?list=PLD7u4sAYcu8qZc2JbDTX_
cc28siMUoNOo

## Video 14 - 32mins

Search youtube - Professor Steve Keen A Real Media Interview
https://youtu.be/l1Gg1RGAO6k

# Fractional lending

Fractional lending is the mechanism whereby the private banks turn a little fiat money into a lot of 'money as debt'.

The *Bank of England* holds the reserve accounts of the 46 private banks who have direct banking facilities there. This is all of the major banks and many of the former building societies. Smaller banks and societies link up with a major bank for B of E facilities.

If a bank has *capital reserves* of £10 billion for instance, then through the process of fractional lending that bank can create around £100 billion of new 'money as debt' in the real economy, nowadays they can do this pretty much for free. Banks pay only a nominal rate of interest to the bank of England for this money making privilege, or sometimes none at all as the government brings in more schemes to encourage borrowing.

Unsurprisingly, this system has led to a massive increase in the levels of debt in our country. It has been the main weapon governments of both colours have used to boost the economy. Our economy is bigger because the amount of debt is greater. How that debt is distributed is extremely important and shapes an economy. Unfortunately, Gordon Brown missed the opportunity to reshape our banking system while he had leverage to do so. Bailing out the banks on the tax payers balance sheet (this money didn't actually exist either remember) without extracting concessions like proscribing lending practices that supported business, GDP growth and personal lending was a bad mistake.

The British banking system is fairly heavily regulated but the allocation of new money as debt is left to the practices and preferences of each individual bank. At the moment, around 80% of new debt goes into...................you guessed it, housing. 17% goes to personal loans such as overdraft and car loans. This leaves 3% for business. Are you shocked by that number? I was, I still am, also a bit angry.

The cost of housing continues to go up and up. The 'cost' is massive. This is a 'double think' scam of epic proportions but we don't get it because we, the homeowner generation, are getting rich, aren't we?

Yes and no. If you buy and hold then yes, you probably are doing well as long as you pay down the mortgage and keep the house habitable. If you move but increase your debt to do so then may not be doing quite so well.

The unseen cost is what economists would call the 'opportunity cost' and the cost to the next generation. The opportunity cost is basically a way of saying, what else could I have done with the money I pay on my mortgage if the house was half the price to begin with? Holidays, a new business, or just managing to have just one salary in the home so we can have our children looked after by one of their parents rather than a state sanctioned nanny. These opportunities are the cost, you decide if you're in profit.

And worse than all that, the cost to the next generation. My parents stole from me.

They didn't mean to of course, certainly not in the literal way, but my parents generation were the first to see massive rises in house prices due to fractional lending and liberated lending practices. The money that they made on their house is paid for by the next generation in absurdly higher house prices. My mother was at home when I was growing up. She went back to work when I was 5 through choice, (good on you Jean). My generation has benefited also, massively but most of us need 2 salaries to enjoy the standard of living we aspire to.

We have stolen from our children. What have we stolen? Their ability to buy a house at all. The lucky ones call on bank of mum and dad but most will not be so lucky. They will either rent or rely on the banks loosening up lending requirements, pump more fake money in and then........ I think you know the rest.

# Banking systems

The rebuilding that was required after the second world war created two very different banking systems, that of the victors and that of the vanquished. Unfortunately our system has been the less effective of the two. The victorious nations carried on much as before, with banks in the UK and USA being able to set their own money as debt allocation priorities. These banks preferred lending into the housing sector which is unencumbered by the limited liability associated with business loans, and is therefore a relatively safe asset. This has created a situation where businesses have struggled to get sufficient loans at competitive rates to finance expansion, new products and technological advances.

Conversely, the rebuilding of the defeated nations of Germany and Japan was carried out under the Marshall plan. The allies had learned a lot from effects of the punishment meted out to Germany after the first world war, effects that eventually lead to the outbreak of the second. Because of this it was seen to be important to help rebuild and create a stable economy rather than punish the defeated states. The Marshall programme concentrated on re building infrastructure, banks and the businesses required to make these countries self sufficient, which was thought to be the most likely way of creating a lasting peace. Peace through trade.

The new banking systems were created with this end in mind. The banks of Japan and Germany's role was to supply funds to industry and promote business generally. What a difference this has made to these economies. The German and Japanese industrial 'miracles' are largely a result of the banks being pro active in the productive part of the economy. Germany still have this foundation.

Few Germans own their own homes so there isn't a massive inflationary effect on prices. Rents therefore are reasonable and most people are happy to rent. Meanwhile, much of the new money that we would throw at houses, the Germans invest in industry and the results are plain. Germany is the powerhouse of the European economy and has the financial and political power that this brings.

In Japan things haven't gone so well. The massive expansion of the Japanese economy had brought a lot of wealth to Japan's businesses and this had started to appear in the workers salaries, but powers within Japan wanted to bring the 'wealth effect' experienced in America under the neoliberal capitalist system.

The neoliberal economic model that we have been following for 4 decades was created by power economist Milton Friedman. His theories of managing an economy by controlling the money supply have been adopted by many western countries. Most famously by Mrs Thatcher and President Ronnie Reagan in the mid 1980's. The financial deregulation that was implemented lead to a fast increase in perceived wealth in America and parts of Britain.

The Bank of Japan wanted to experiment with the neoliberal economic model and mostly abandoned the banking structure created by the Marshall plan. The financialisation of the Japanese economy led to a massive boom in land and equity prices and then the subsequent collapse seen in the early '90s that they are still struggling to come out of.

## Video 15 - 1 hour 32 mins

Youtube search - Princes of the yen.
https://youtu.be/p5Ac7ap_MAY

This film depicts beautifully how financial policy and mis management can affect a country. We saw the rise of Japan as an industrial nation and this film explains the banking policies that has led to a near 30 year stagnation.

Japanese central banks had a system known as 'window guidance' which guided the private banks to not only lend a certain amount into the economy, but also stipulated the industry sectors that would receive this new money. This system contributed to the massive growth of Japanese industry. Because their focus was on industry, the populace didn't necessarily feel the 'wealth effect' that they saw in America. This wealth effect would require a shift towards lending to individuals, promoting stock market and property speculation. The bank of Japan swapped focus to force the development of a speculative bubble?! I know, crazy, but if you watched the film I'm pretty sure you will see that this is what happened.

It's becoming clear that the neoliberal economic doctrine that Japan, the USA and UK currently follow, only works for the banking sector. Astonishingly, this doctrine doesn't take account of debt money, the money private banks create. The money supply as represented by the central bank capital accounts is the only money supply this theory wishes to regulate but the fact that it takes no account of private debt leaves a massive hole in the calculations for the monetary effects on the whole economy.

Professor Steve Keen is really good on this as is Professor Michael Hudson and Professor Mark Blyth. Look these guys up on youtube.

# Tax

There a few things more political than tax.

The first iteration of a formal income tax system was introduced by William Pitt in 1798 to raise the money needed to fight the French, specifically Napoleon Bonaparte. We beat Napoleon but the long term price was tax on our pay.

It was meant to be a temporary measure, but you guessed it, the government rather liked all this new money (power) they had and now taxes are as certain as death.

The word tax is derived from the latin 'Taxare' which meant something more like appraise. So the word's meaning developed from the process of deciding what you had to pay and has since become the word used to describe the payment itself. Tax has also now taken on the connotation of something that is onerous. Quelle surprise?

Our government spends around 43% of total GDP. Some people represent this by what day in the calendar we have created enough money to have 'paid' for our governance for that year. This is known as the 'Tax Freedom Day' and the later in the year this day falls, the greater the overall tax burden must have been. In 2015 Tax Freedom Day was the 3rd of June, this year, tax freedom day was four days later in the calendar.

The state of our tax legislation and practices of the inland revenue are probably the most divisive and damaging aspect of our economic system today. Worse even than the conduct and regulation of the banks.

For a start, our tax laws are massive, some 17,000 pages long. The way that modern tax law is written is one of the worst abuses of power that I can think of. The government uses the large accountancy and law firms to write the legislation and these same firms will then use their knowledge of the finer details to advise their clients on 'back door' ways to get around. Companies and individuals unable to hire extremely expensive tax advisers are locked into paying these same taxes.

The big four accountancy firms, KPMG, Deloitte, PriceWaterhouseCoopers and Ernst and Young are said to be behind almost all of the offshoring schemes and manipulations of the tax system which our legislation permits and only the very wealthy can afford to make the most of this opportunity. The loss of tax revenue is made up by higher nominal taxes for the worker bees and a higher debt load for the young and yet to be born.

### Video 16 - 53 mins - Jaw dropping.

Youtube search - Taxodus - Playing The Global Tax Avoidance Game
https://youtu.be/tvlLO_pTmeY?list=PLD7u4sAYcu8qZc2Jb
DTX_cc28siMUoNOo

Another problem with the international tax system is the competitive nature of setting corporate tax rates. On the one hand, countries are reducing their corporate tax rate to encourage more businesses to domicile for tax. America's tax rate is 35% plus a state tax, while the UK is currently 19% and set to fall to 15%. This creates a big problem for America as so many companies which have a natural home in the States, don't send any of their foreign earned profits there. Apple are sat on a cash pile worth over $200 billion which they can't pay to their shareholders without incurring a huge tax bill as they take the money home.

On the other hand, reducing taxes without getting rid of the tax loopholes, means it's almost guaranteed that the tax income from the corporate sector will continue to reduce. This ultimately means that we, the worker bees are still tapped for the difference.

## Types of tax

We have so many different forms of taxation now. Tax on employment (labour), tax on consumption via VAT and fuel taxes, taxes on capital via capital gains and taxes on death. The government has it covered. The vast array of taxes and the way they are applied means that we all have a different blend of taxes that we pay, and for worker bees there are no legal ways of avoiding them.

Taxes on consumption are relatively fair as you can choose whether or not to buy a certain item or service. Value Added Tax (VAT) is applied to many goods and services but there are exemptions such as basic foods and children's clothing. For the poorer in a society, food will form a major part of their budget and they will therefore pay relatively little VAT. More affluent people will pay a higher level of VAT as their consumption of luxury goods and services increases. In this way, VAT is somewhat fairly apportioned.

## Who pays income tax?

Government workers don't pay tax. If you are a government worker this might come as a shock, because you do see tax on your pay slip after all. The reality is that your employer and the taxman are the same entity, so although you see a deduction, it doesn't add to the exchequer, it merely reduces the net loss. There are all sorts of slightly 'ins' and 'outs' to that as mentioned below, but in principle, this is true. Government employees don't pay tax, they are tax. Sorry again, but this is something that needs to be understood especially with the high wages and pensions so many public sector workers benefit from. This is another strong argument for decreased direct government spending and increasing true privatisation and competition for government services.

New tax income can only come from the private sector working on privately funded projects. By this rationale, a private firm being paid by the government makes no immediate contribution to the exchequer either but does divert the pension liability away from the public purse. For a company or individual to contribute to a country's tax income the paymaster and customer must be outside government.

Much of the income for the government is tax that has been recycled and does not therefore constitute new income. As the public sector grows, the level of tax recycling is almost certainly growing as well.

Public sector workers like teachers or nurses retiring with a pension of £25,000 a year, have a virtual pension pot of at least £750,000 at current annuity rates. This is far, far more than most private sector workers with comparable salaries can save for their pensions. Estimates of the average pension pot in the UK vary, but none get above £90,000. Most estimates are in the £50,000 range which will currently allow a pension of around £2,200 per year. Unlike public sector pensions, this figure isn't index linked. Index linking a £50,000 annuity will drop the income below £2000.

The government also still lets many of it's employees retire very early, at a time when private sector workers have seen their retirement age go up to 67.

These public sector perks are mostly unfunded so the people who ultimately pay for them are future generations working in private industries through their taxes, and increased debt. Private sector pensions are mostly funded, ie people and companies save money so they don't create an increased, 'off balance sheet' debt burden in the same way.

Government debt can be seen as current debt only (£1.6 trillion) or, more accurately as debt already accrued plus future obligations like government employee pensions. These are 'off balance sheet' and are therefore invisible but are a very real burden. The Office of National Statistics estimates that this off balance sheet debt for pensions alone stands at £7.1 Trillion.

## Tax Recycling

Imagine you own a cafe. Because of the position of you cafe, the main customers come from the office blocks near by. One is a government department and one is the head office of a supermarket chain. On the money you receive from these different groups, on which you will eventually pay tax, only the supermarket's employees will offer new tax income, via you, to the treasury. The money spent by the employees of the government department is purely tax recycling as they've seen this money before at HMRC. They're pleased to see it back of course, but it ain't new.

Deeper - how much of the income from the supermarket is derived from employees of the government shopping within their stores? Government workers consume goods and services within the private sector, so there is also an element of tax recycling here as well.

Deeper - If your cafe does really well, you may eventually grow sufficiently to join the big boys and start offshoring your profits. Now the amount of taxes being recycled is greatly reduced. Much of the profits stop going back to the government as taxes and are sent for a rest in the Caymen islands or Panama instead.

Deeper - As the spending habits of consumers gravitates towards the big brand players, offshoring of profits and non payment of tax in the country of operation drains the tax take again- and recycling is further curtailed.

Deeper - The companies offshoring profits gather a tax free war chest which enables them to buy up possible competition, suppliers and emerging technology firms. Google are now known as Alphabet as they have bought so many new firms with their tax free money that they chose a more inclusive corporate identity. I'm sure all the potential profits of the firms taken over will also now be offshored.

Deepest - The government's inability to write fair tax law and impose it equally entrenches the advantage and power of the big corporates, I think the government understands this very well and have done nothing to correct this unjust system. When government and corporate interests are aligned, we, the worker bees have to work and be taxed in their service. Some people, careful now......... might say........that this is a soft form of fascism. We are put to work to protect the matrix of government and big business.

Tax is very political.

Tax legislation is broken.

Tax reform is impossible without a change of personnel.

# Taxation of capital and labour

One of the defining features of our taxation system is the difference between the way labour and capital are treated.

Labour – Income tax is the largest contributor to the inland revenue of all the taxes. As we, the worker bees, work and earn money in exchange for our labour, the government extracts taxes from the accrued salaries. We have two main taxes on labour, income tax and national insurance.

The name of the tax really makes no difference, the net effect of the two taxes together creates a large reduction on the disposable incomes available to us to elect to spend on the things we value or need.

Employers are also having to face greater taxes paid per employee. An employer pays national insurance contributions and now they also obliged to make a contribution to the personal pension schemes of their staff. Taxes are a drag on capital but are also a disincentive to employing more people. Taxes on people last for the duration of their employment where as, an investment in advanced machines and robotics doesn't carry such a large long term extra cost.

Capital – The way capital is taxed is very different and is open to far more manipulation due to the liquidity of money. For the purposes of taxation, capital is money held as profits, savings or gains on investments. Capital is the surplus that individuals and businesses create from within the economy.

For individuals, capital is the profit from their labour, for business, it is often the profit from other people's labour. The two are not mutually exclusive, for example a premiership footballer is an employee but since the earn such huge sums, this allows them to accrue a large excess which they can then invest. (The irony is that many of the clubs that employ them, manage to lose money).

Many people employed in the financial sector are also very high earners, often receiving large bonuses so being an employee doesn't mean you can't enjoy the benefits of capital.

I worked in a dental laboratory that was part owned by my father until I bought his share and eventually bought out my partner. This allowed me to gain sufficient capital (retained profits) to buy a commercial building and a CAD/CAM facility. I have transitioned from being totally reliant on my labour for income as I now also have an income from my capital (CAD/CAM production and rent on the building). This is a good example of how capitalism can work, I have enough customers who choose to use my services, that gives me a profit. I have chosen to use this profit to invest in assets that will bring me further income.

In my opinion, the taxation system is the most corrupting and unfair mechanism in our economy. The wide difference between the taxes on labour and capital are totally unjustifiable. I suspect the younger generations will eventually revolt against this system if we, the invested generations, don't vote to change it first.

This may sound like a socialist manifesto, but I can assure you that I am a capitalist at heart and I would like more people to have some freedom to be capitalist as well. We can only gain those freedoms if we have the opportunity to earn and then spend much more of our own money. This requires far lower taxes overall and much less government intervention on spending. Remember, we are all participating capitalists in the sense that we make choices on where we spend our money. To have more freedom and better services we need to be able to buy them from visibly competitive businesses and I truly believe that the vast majority of people are capable of making good choices. Imagine how it must feel if you are poor in today's society. The government makes so many choices on your behalf and you have little disposable income to make your own priorities count. We have many good services, but all of them could be delivered better, cheaper and more locally if the government allowed some open competition.

## Tax reform

The first thing I believe we need to do to create a fairer society is to make taxes on labour and capital the same. I wouldn't say without exceptions, but any exception needs to be written in a paragraph of text that a person of average intelligence can understand.

For instance, let's start with a rate of 15%. Income tax is 15%, capital gains tax is 15% tax on interest is 15%, death duties are 15%. Hardest of all, capital gains on houses would also be 15%.

I know, this is big deal, but remember, you didn't earn this money, it was given to you by the Bank of England increasing the money supply and encouraging asset prices to rise. The overall effect of this, I think, would be to end the acceleration of house prices due to monetary inflation. There would be a very difficult period as we, the addicts, would have to get used to seeing our homes as a place to live and less as an investment vehicle. This is the only way that the housing market can be made to function for all (or as close to 100% as we can get).

The price of houses would drop as people's expectations come back into line with what is affordable. Younger people would then have a better choice between renting or owning. Advanced countries like Germany have a population that mostly rents and there is no reason the UK couldn't be the same.

The government creates the 'wealth effect' that is rising house prices, but ultimately we don't often get to see that profit as when we sell one house we normally have to buy another one. In addition there is the opportunity cost of devoting so much money to houses. When the first of the £44,000 university debt generation get into power (2035 ish) do you think they, will go light on us?

The power of HMRC is also a very worrying aspect of the growth of government power. They can shut down a business if they suspect that taxes have not been properly calculated and paid. The onus is then on the business concerned to prove they were right. This is the reverse of our legal system, 'innocent until proven guilty'. Of course, HMRC would only use these tactics on smaller businesses who can't 'lawyer up' like the big boys.

Getting rid of taxes like VAT makes administration easier and authoritarian regulation and control mostly redundant. The removal or reduction of VAT rates would allow people to consume products and services at a lower cost.

All administrative burdens, tax included, fall most heavily on the small to medium businesses. Large businesses and multinational corporates can afford to have whole departments devoted to aspects of compliance such as tax and tax avoidance. This has become more and more true as the level of red tape has increased. It has had the effect of entrenching the advantage of the big boys at the expense of smaller businesses that may have many advantages over the incumbent market leader. It's high time we had a three or four page tax law, closed the HMRC and started again with a new administrative body whose job would be to police self assessment tax returns by business and individuals that are outside of the PAYE system.

One of the perceived problems with our current system is that many of the largest companies pay the least tax, and this, is partly true. Multinationals in particular have a built in advantage in their ability to 'offshore' their profits through legal accounting practices. The 'double Irish with a Dutch sandwich' is one such scheme. Ireland and Holland amongst others, encourage businesses to be domiciled in their country by offering low rates of corporation tax and certain loose regulations that allow the diversion of profits away from the country where they are generated.

Starbucks, along with many other international and national businesses, reduce their UK tax bill by booking activity through an offshore company. They do this by dividing sales between different nominal codes including intangibles like brand value. A £2.50 cup of coffee could be said to have a higher value because it's a 'Starbucks' coffee. If their brand is registered offshore, they can then assign a portion of each sale to that company so that 'brand' appears as a cost in the accounts even though it's a nebulous item, hard to value.

Another tactic is to have suppliers owned by your company but again registered in a low tax jurisdiction. In this way, Starbucks can effectively charge themselves a heavy sum for their coffee ingredients and again, this will appear as a cost and not therefore subject to UK tax.

The double Irish scheme takes this offshored profit through an Irish registered 'shell' company and then does the same process through a Dutch 'shell' before coming back to Ireland to pay a very small amount of tax in a third 'shell'. (A 'shell' company is a subsidiary of the main company, usually with no employees. They are set up purely for the purpose of minimising tax)

In the recent EU court case against Google, it was estimated that they have been paying around 1% tax in Dublin on all their European and South Asia business. In Britain where Google had paid no tax until recently being shamed into it. They were able to do a 'sweetheart' deal with HMRC for

£130m for 10 years tax. They are only able to do a deal like this because they have better lawyers than you or I, and because the laws are so badly written (17,000 pages) that it's easier for the taxman to roll over.

## Video 17 - 8 mins

Youtube search - Apple's dirty little tax secret - APPLE NEWS
https://youtu.be/zKFFCga7T9w

It's easy to point the finger at these American multinationals but UK businesses are doing the same as well, especially the banks who have a myriad of offshore schemes to avoid paying their taxes as well as extending this service to their wealthier clients tax affairs.

These schemes exists because of the tax law. It's not the fault of the businesses themselves, although we all can see that they don't conduct themselves in the spirit of the law. When I have had a chance to legally reduce the amount of tax I pay, I have taken it. I believe most people would.

A move to a low but uniform tax rate seems to me to be a good thing. The other side of this equation though is that the tax law needs to be totally rewritten so that all businesses actually pay 15% tax on their profits. A tax code of a few pages that contains just a few minor exceptions to any tax would remove the motivation to try and get out of paying taxes and would also put thousands of tax lawyers and civil servants out of work. They could then hopefully find productive work within the new businesses that can better compete with their larger rivals.

## Higher rate tax?

Higher rates of tax, especially income tax are often seen as a method of wealth distribution and can certainly have that effect. However studies and experience have shown that the more punitive levels, over 50% for instance, will actually have a negative effect on total tax receipts. Within the current system, the cost of collecting higher tax rates is also relatively high as people subject to these taxes use exotic schemes to avoid them. HMRC can easily spend more on recovery than the value of the tax actually recovered and so not all the receipts go through to investment favouring the poorer parts of the community.

With a more uniform tax structure where individuals and businesses pay tax on labour and capital at the same rate, the tax collection should be far simpler and more effective but the natural political system of imposing higher rates on the wealthy is unlikely to change. I don't think that a higher rate is necessarily a negative thing for the economy as many successful countries in Europe and beyond have rates in the 40-55% range.

With uniform taxation of labour and capital at a higher rate I can imagine that the actual tax receipts would be very good even if that rate is lower than many other countries. A rate of 30% on salaries or capital gains shouldn't have the effect of encouraging people to avoid this higher level as is the case with, what can be seen by the people paying them, as unfair rates of 50% and above.

# Invisible Tax

Another type of tax which we don't see is the loss of value due to inflation. Nowadays central banks are printing so much money to expand the money supply with the aim of promoting growth. Despite the lack of inflation as expressed by the CPI, it's very likely that at some point we will see this go up. As I will discuss later, it's questionable whether CPI is an honest reflection of inflation as experienced by worker bees, but the fact that inflation makes things more expensive means that in effect your money has lost purchasing power. As this inflation is government policy you could, and should see this as a tax on your spending power and savings.

This practice is also known as 'currency debasement'. This policy of taxation by inflation mostly affects savers and pensioners to the benefit of borrowers and the government who devalue their debt through the same inflationary process.

Another form of monetary taxation is the effect policy has on the savings and pensions of citizens. The very low interest rates we have means that there is almost nowhere that a good, safe rate of return can be made. This has the effect of reducing future income from these savings.

People working within the private sector are obliged to save more income into their pension schemes to try and give a decent income in retirement. The combined effect of inflation and low interest rates makes this an extremely difficult task.

# Trusted Third Parties

The use of gold as a currency created the banks and banking. These private companies are known as trusted third parties (TTP). In the early banking system, banks would print their own paper notes as currency and the bank would be a trusted third party between people using their currency. People who used bank notes would trust that the gold actually existed in the vaults and that they could collect it if necessary, by redeeming the note, and move it to another bank if they so wished. Banks were regional so people who moved around would sometimes want to physically move their gold to another bank, another currency. The increasing use of bank notes as the only form of exchange relied on these trusted banks to mediate between buyers and sellers, depositors and borrowers. It all comes down to trust.

In our modern system where so many transactions are purely digital, TTP's are more important than ever. In the UK we now have around 30 national banks as well as former building societies turned banks (ie, have the ability to create money as debt rather than lending money from depositors). We also have many credit card providers associated with these and other foreign banks and institutions. These are all trusted third parties who facilitate the movement of all the digital money within our system. The movement of money within these TTP networks creates 'friction' to transactions in the form of fees and time.

All transaction using digital money will incur a loss of time and money to the trusted third parties. A simple bank transfer can take a couple of days or more all though this is improving. The sheer number of transactions means that all this money being 'held' by the banks for a short time, adds up to a lot of money. It would be like having a large lake that is fed by a stream and drained by a similar stream, the bank takes and gives the stream of money but it holds the lake. This lake of money can be used by the bank to make money. This has created scandal at times for the banks for example with the LIBOR rigging in the 2000's and overnight trading schemes, so called 'bed and breakfasting'.

With credit and debit card payments there are fees paid by the merchants to the companies who clear these transactions. If the account isn't cleared in full each month, there is also a heavy penalty in the form of interest charged to the customer at around 30%, or 600 times the base rate at the moment.

International money transfer is another expensive problem for some people. If a migrant worker in the UK wishes to send money home to help support their family, this involves moving this money to a different currency and across international banking facilities. The friction in these type of transactions can be punitive. A few days can elapse before the money shows up in the recipient's account and the financial cost will be two fold. Normally there will be a fee or commission paid to the bank or financial intermediaries. There will also be a difference in the currency exchange rate that is applied to the sender compared to the rate applied to the intermediary (spread). The overall cost of this type of international, inter currency transfer could easily be 10-20%.

One of the possible developments of our money systems is likely to be a move to currencies with less friction. The use of air time in Kenya as a currency means that this is a form of digital currency. If the mobile operator works in several countries, the use of this credit as a currency could facilitate frictionless cross border trade. This is very close to what *crypto currencies* offer. More on them later.

The mobile operators are not specifically set up to be banks or financial organisations but have, never the less become a trusted third party in this ad hoc currency. The fact that air time is paid for in advance means that it is also, largely, a debt free system. The problem here is that the possibility of the mobile operator going out of business is higher than with a bank as banks tend to get bailed out by government.

As more and more of our everyday transactions become purely digital, we are more open to money systems that will be instant and without any financial penalty. If we used trusted third parties who allowed the transfer of currency between users without time or financial penalty, we could see a much more liberal economy develop. If money transfer was free and instant a whole new micro economy could emerge where money moved between suppliers of goods, and particularly of services in a new way. Competition would ensure that we could start to pay for less waste and more of exactly what we want. For instance, we could pay for micro services over the internet, and pay for exactly the amount of a service we consume, down to fractions of a penny.

Our current system tends to extract money from an increasing number of transactions. I still use cash in the pub and when shopping around town, coffee shops or buying lunch, but I'm a dinosaur. Younger consumers tend to use a card payment for many of these smaller transactions. Fees are being paid on more and more of our purchases, which favours the banks and credit card companies and forces smaller retailers and service providers to sign up with trusted third parties to provide the digital services they wouldn't have needed before.

I expect new players like Amazon or Paypal for instance will come into this TTP market to launch their own branded digital currency some day soon. A global, trusted third party who will act as a bank, so fees will be paid to compensate the provider for all the infrastructure required, but these fees are likely to be much smaller than the cumbersome banking system we have now.

If you got paid in "Amazons" for instance, think how many of your purchases you could make with them? Clothes and consumer goods, no problem. Amazon are in the fresh food market too. Amazons could be accepted by major Amazon partners like Cinema chains, Domino pizza or even Tesco. You could buy sterling or dollars on Amazon as well for home delivery. If a third of your salary was paid in Amazons, would you pay tax on it? What about two thirds?? If you get a 5% discount by using amazons, this would be akin to getting 5% interest on you balance, this is a very good return by today's standards.

These are the sort of scenarios we are likely to be facing within five years as our old debt based money comes under attack. Expect the banks and our government to put up a big fight to retain the status quo though. The government especially need to maintain total control of 'money' so they can collect taxes efficiently.

This could be a stepping stone to a true crypto currency where there is no TTP involved. I would highly recommend reading 'Bitcoin' by Domonic Frisby if this concept interests you. This book will explain the links to currency, cryptography and the block chain. That, as they say, is the future

# Bonds

When the government needs to borrow money they do so by issuing bonds which in a rather fancy way, the UK government calls 'Guilts'. The US has a more workmanlike name for their bonds, Treasury notes.

A bond is essentially an IOU on fixed terms. To receive money from the banks, the government creates these bonds with a maturity date and an associated interest rate and the banks accepts these IOU's as collateral on the loan.

The bond holder receives the interest payments (sometimes called the 'coupon'), normally two payments per year, at the rate the bond was issued. These payments continue at this fixed rate until the date the bond matures. When the bond matures the government repays the principal to the bondholder and the asset and liability cancel each other out and this money disappears (removed from the balance sheet).

When the government needs more money (always) they give new bonds to the B of E to sell. It then holds an auction with invited institutions to buy the guilts for their investment portfolios, pensions and the like. The B of E has an advantage here because the government has passed laws forcing many financial institutions to hold a certain level of bonds within their portfolio. How cool is that? No choice in the free market way, no, you have to own our paper.

Only certain banks and institutions are invited to bid at auction and then they can place the guilts on the secondary market making a tidy profit for themselves. This is where smaller players and other nation states can buy these bonds.

The secondary bond market sets the current prices of bonds and therefore the *yield*. This secondary market did, and should have a real impact on interest rates set by the central banks.

If a bond is issued at a 2% interest rate for instance but the country concerned is seen to be becoming a higher risk, this should have the effect of reducing bond prices to reflect the greater risk (prices down mean yield goes up). In this case, a 10 year bond initially sold for £1000 may end up selling for only £500 for instance. The interest paid to the bondholder is still the same 2% but as the latest owner has paid only half the original amount, the yield for him is now 4%.

This country's central bank will now need to sell new bonds at a similar price in order get new funds as no rational trader will buy a newly issued 10 year maturing bond at 2% when he can buy an 8 year maturing bond at 4%. Therefore, most governments have to follow the secondary bond market rate to continue to receive new loans.

That's basically how it should work.

But *quantitative easing* (more on this soon) has changed that for now as governments, particularly Japan at the moment, are having their own central bank buy all their own bonds. Freakonomics!

Countries with central banks have this bond issuance. These are known as sovereign bonds.

The sovereign bond market is also very important for world trade. Having a large 'liquid' market (meaning easy to buy and sell on demand) for currency based bonds facilitates trade as a country who holds large amounts of foreign currency through trade surplus, (think Japan or China), can use surplus currency to buy an investment with yield (interest). The interest earned on the bonds, helps to protect themselves against inflation within that currency which would otherwise have the effect of devaluing their holdings of foreign reserves.

For example, if you were to bring home some currency from a foreign holiday and hold onto it knowing you are going back there in a couple of years. You know, it just gets left in a drawer with the passports. When you return to this destination to spend your local currency, if prices there have doubled, you have effectively lost half of your money. Countries holding billions or trillions of foreign currency can't afford this risk so instead of holding cash, they buy bonds. Sovereign bond yield (interest) tend to reflect the underlying conditions of a country's economic performance, a country with high inflation is likely to pay higher interest so if you are able to hold bonds rather than cash, you are likely to lose far less of your purchasing power.

The dollar in particular has benefited from this phenomenon, Japan and then China were buying huge amounts of Treasury notes which helped to allow America to run equally huge deficits. The UK also benefits from the status of the pound as a reserve currency (for now).

Businesses also use bond issuance to fund their capital expenditure, expansions or take overs. Large corporations can benefit from lower rates offered by bonds than are available from the banks. The corporate bonds find there way into banks, funds, insurance companies and are now often owned by central banks. They are not generally available to 'retail' investors (worker bees) except if wrapped within a fund or trust product from a bank or insurance company.

Corporate bonds are often referred to as 'junk bonds' which considering the state of some national finances, seems more than a little unfair!

Smaller businesses often use bonds to get finance that our recalcitrant banks refuse. For instance some smaller businesses may issue bonds direct to retail investors, businesses like Innis & Gunn Brewery. They offered higher interest returns if you took payment in beer! Wasps rugby club raised money to buy their new stadium partly with a retail bond offering.

As the banks fail to support businesses, more companies needing finance look outside the banking system and go off grid or on line. This is where the private equity and 'peer to peer' lending companies have developed so much in the last few years. A small company can borrow from savers through a trusted third party, in return both parties get better rates of interest than the banks are offering. This is a very positive outcome for the way our financial markets work and we are likely to see many new initiatives that cut the banks out and innovate new trusted third party players such as Funding Circle, Zopa and Ratesetter.

# The Bank of England

The B of E is a quasi nationalised but politically independent institution. This means that it runs monetary policy for the UK via the Governor, currently Mark Carney, with the Monetary Policy Committee meeting monthly to decide on interest rates and issues around the money supply. They have also introduced a policy called Quantitative Easing since the 2007/8 crisis.

The money supply is the amount of money put into the economy via the private banks. The bank of England can influence the money supply by the amount of 'fiat' money it issues as capital reserves.

The policy framework that the B of E is meant to adhere to is to provide money to the government via the issuance of gilts, manage capital accounts of the private banking sector, ensure stability of the pound in international markets and to manage the money supply to create an inflation rate of 2%.

I thought the creation of an independent Bank of England was a sensible move, as did many others at the time. Governments in the past had tinkered with interest rates to achieve political ends, these experiments with governments controlling both fiscal and monetary policy often backfired, so we were given a fully independent governor in 2008.

The prevailing economic theory of the time, as it is still, is the neoliberal school that favours the creation of an independent central bank to oversee money creation. Gordon Brown's time with the 'Bilderberg Group' where the global elites plan the world economy may have influenced his decision to follow this path.

Most people are unfamiliar with the Bilderberg's but they are a very influential group of bankers, industrialists, media, military and political power brokers and unlike Davos, it's very secret.

## Video 18 - 25 mins

Youtube search - Bilderberg Group: The Secret Rulers of the World
https://youtu.be/HBypAFQ3ZCk

# Capital Reserves

Capital reserves are fiat monies. The Bank of England holds this money which is guaranteed by the ability of the government to raise money through taxation. The amount of money in reserves will put an upper limit on the amount of money as debt that is in the economy at any time. The level of capital reserves creates an upper limit via fractional lending but it does not guarantee that all this money feeds into the real economy. This is due to the way banks allocate their resources.

Capital accounts in the B of E are a mechanism for controlling debt and also monetary inflation. Capital account money doesn't leave the B of E, it's merely moved between the 46 accounts to reflect daily movements between banks. When the end of day accounting is done at the B of E only the net amounts are moved between the banks, the total available capital reserve will remain unchanged.

If 50 customers of bank A buy houses from customers of bank B, but on the same day, 40 customers of bank B buy houses from bank A customers, only the net difference needs to move. The net amount to be moved between the capital accounts of these banks will depend on the relative prices.

When a bank comes under pressure because of bad news regarding their financial health, it is the capital reserve that will save or sink them. For retail investors concerned about their bank, the obvious strategy is to queue up at the bank and demand cash at the counter, possibly emptying their 'demand accounts'. Cash is pretty scarce in any advanced economy so this would quickly force any bank to halt cash withdrawals. This alone doesn't mean the bank is insolvent. After withdrawing cash, the next most sensible strategy for customers is to have the money represented in their accounts moved to an alternative 'safe' institution. This is when the capital accounts can really come under pressure. As money from the embattled bank is transferred to other institutions, the bank's capital account will begin to empty and the tipping point comes quickly as the amount of debt the bank holds doesn't drop at the rate the reserves are being lost. In a crisis, the amount of debt may be going up as it did with Northern Rock.

Under fractional lending practices, a bank must hold a certain level of reserves against the outstanding debt on their balance sheet. As the reserves drop, at some point they would be technically bankrupt. They may still have massive reserve money, just not massive enough relative to outstanding debt. At this point, the bank should be dead.

What often happens then is a bank rescue, either through other banks lending capital reserves back to the troubled bank, or as in 2008, the government pumps lots of new capital reserve money in via the Bank of England. Don't panic, remember, none of this 'money' actually exists, it's an accounting game.

The fiat money within the B of E never touches the real economy, it is there as an accounting mechanism. Practically all the money that touches our lives is created by the commercial banks and is therefore debt 'backed' by fiat money. Remember that without a system that is backed by gold or other commodity backed system, fiat money only exists as a government IOU.

The only fiat money that is in the real economy are the notes and coins printed and minted by the Bank of England which accounts for only 3% of the total money supply, furthermore only a small percentage of that 3% is actually in circulation at any one time.

One of the problems governments are having is getting enough money into areas of the economy that will boost *Gross Domestic Product* (GDP). This is mainly because they haven't introduced a mechanism to force banks to lend to small and medium enterprises (SME's) which tend to be the real force behind growth in earnings, productivity, innovation and employment. The government can boost public spending but the emphasis lately has rather been to get individuals to increase their borrowing (leverage) so that the government can begin the process of reducing theirs. As stated before, both the government and private sector cannot deleverage at the same time, we have to take it in turns to be up to eyes in it or there will be a damaging recession. More on recession later.

# Inflation

What is inflation? Nowadays inflation is reported as the largely arbitrary number called Consumer Price Index (CPI). This government controlled statistic is made up of a virtual basket of everyday goods and services. It's designed (allegedly) to reflect the price increase, or decrease, in the cost of living. You can find the list on the Office of National Statistics web site.

One of the last straws of 'news' that kicked me into writing this book was a report on the CPI figure for the previous month, June 2016. The news report was that 'CPI has jumped from 01% to 0.3% partly due to the price of some apps'! House or rental prices through the roof but an app goes from 69p to £1.20 and that's stoking inflation. 1984.

According to the ONS we are all spending slightly more on eating out in restaurants each month than the total cost of housing including mortgage or rent, utility bills and maintenance. According to them, the average spend on housing in 2015 was £158.30 a week or £46.60 if utility bills are excluded. I will leave you to decide if this is a fair reflection of worker bee spending but in contrast, thisismoney.co.uk estimate the countries renters spend, on average 41% of their income on housing.

Of course the statistics are a reflection of the fact that according to the ONS report in 2008/10, only 37.3% of households had a mortgage with an average value of £75,000 each. It also stated that 92% of the poorest fifth of the population rent, whereas only 3.2% of the wealthiest fifth do. It would be hard not to argue then that the government's chosen inflation statistic favours the rich and older population over the poorer, younger worker bees.

CPI is the index used for the 2% target for inflation set by the government which the current governor has struggled so much to meet. He is obliged to write a letter to the Chancellor of the Exchequer to explain himself when this is missed. He's written a lot of letters.

The CPI has been used for inflation reporting since 2006, before that we had Retail Price Index (RPI) which is a little closer to reality. This does better reflect some of the major costs incurred in real life but it's still unreliable as it doesn't fully address the cost of housing, services and of course government. RPI was swapped to CPI when inflation was looking bad for government. Inflation eventually fell and now the B of E is struggling to get the headline rate back to 2% because the items and weighting within the virtual basket are designed to suppress inflation by over representing prices of things that technology and globalisation hold down.

Big items not included in the official government inflation figure is government itself. The inflation within the NHS for instance has been a lot higher than the CPI rate for years. This increase in pricing isn't felt by people as we are not having to pay directly.

Inflation is caused by several factors such as demand, the price of imports, cost of production or the amount of money in circulation. The *velocity* at which money moves through the economy is also associated with inflation/deflation depending on whether money is moving around faster or slower.

# Monetary inflation

Inflation used to refer solely to an increase in the money supply. Inflation was how much more money there was in a financial system. This was easy to understand when our economy was on the gold standard. All money was represented by gold to some extent. As the amount of gold increased, banks would issue more money into the system. This was inflation.

This new money entering the economy could cause prices to increase if a commensurate increase in goods and services on offer was not achieved. It's the appearance of new money that forces prices to rise when this money doesn't enter the economy due to greater activity.

As I mentioned right at the beginning of the book, an increase in the total amount of money in the economy (money supply) will increase the prices for which a number of items, beautiful houses on the hill, can be sold for. If however, the money supply doubles but so does the total supply of 'things' like houses on the hill, prices should remain relatively constant.

The lack of visible inflation is due to the fact that the new money entering into the economy is being directed at parts of the economy not reflected in the CPI figure. Housing (mostly), shares, art, vintage cars etc and government. This new money is looking for speculative investment opportunity or is being spent by government on whatever schemes they fancy. For instance, the latest estimate for refurbishing the house of commons is, wait for it.........................6-7 thousand million pounds. The entire 2012 Olympic games cost 8.77 billion but somehow, our representatives in government are going to spend at least £6 billion on one building???!!!!

This inflation reduces the value of money you have, the money you earn and, if you can't afford a second home for investment purposes, it also increases the aggregate percentage of income spent on housing.

Only the wealthy are insulated from this inflation of the money supply caused by banks fractional reserve lending and quantitative easing. Only the wealthy have gained from this process.

As I mentioned earlier, globalisation has brought very strong deflationary pressures as 'things' we buy become progressively cheaper through innovation, competition and lower labour costs. Things that we buy within the retail sector are reducing in price and increasing in quality almost without exception. (The ONS uses a little trick called 'hedonic adjustment' to further massage the inflation numbers. 'Hedonic' refers to the improvement in quality that we enjoy for instance original clunky car phone to today's smartphone).

This innovation and competition also works on our food supply through supermarkets buying produce from the cheapest suppliers anywhere in the world as is also the case for gadgets and wetsuits.

The areas that are inflating are the government sector like council tax rates, the regulated sector, NHS, rail fares for example and corporates/ utilities such as TV and water.

Why is the gap between rich and poor growing? It's partly due to the fact that real inflation is the increase in the money supply. CPI is a sticking plaster to keep the masses nice and quiet while the rich and government run off with the money.

If the real inflation figure were just 2% higher (a modest estimate of reality in my opinion), then the UK has been in a slump recession since 2008. I think this is the case. We are turning Japanese.

# Deflation

Deflation is the opposite to inflation, it's a contraction of the money supply and the reduction of prices that this might cause. When money is extracted from the economy through mechanisms like high interest rates, higher taxes or commodity price inflation, people and institutions will try to preserve their purchasing power by finding cheaper alternatives to their existing purchase options.

If you earn £2500 a month, but a tax increase reduces this to £2,300 you have two options. Maintain your current purchasing preferences but cut out £200 worth of consumption or find enough new, cheaper alternative products to buy so that you maintain the same level of consumption but for a lower price.

This process will cause the providers of more expensive produce, that is being abandoned in favour of cheaper alternatives, to try and reduce their prices to regain market share.

We are seeing this deflationary pressure in the supermarket industry with Aldi and Lidl gaining market share at the expense of the mid to high market stores like Sainsbury's and Waitrose.

As well as interest rates and tax, monetary deflation also happens as a result of more people deleveraging (paying off debt) than are leveraging (going into debt). This, as mentioned before, is why students are being put into increasing debt levels, to compensate for people in the baby boomer age group who are paying off their mortgages and paying for stuff with savings rather than debt.

Japan have been in a deflationary cycle for a couple of decades due to extreme versions of these debt and demographic problems. Although the Bank of Japan has been running a massive quantitative easing program, putting trillions of yen into the economy, there is still little sign of inflation. It's the entrenched deflation and lack of appetite for debt amongst the ageing population that means no upward movement in CPI inflation.

## Video 19 - 30 mins

Youtube search - Top 4 reasons for deflation - Hidden secrets of money - Ep. 6 Mike Maloney

https://youtu.be/8GP87dgTqF8?list=PLE88E9ICdipidHkTehs1VbFzgwrq1jkUJ

# Velocity

The faster money moves, the more GDP it creates, and this will generally lead to higher inflation.

As a note is exchanged for goods and services, it would be theoretically possible for five people to spend the same fiver during the same day. I pay for a taxi to work, the taxi driver pays for some petrol, the petrol station owner buys lunch but breaks a tooth, he pays me the fiver to fix his denture and I pay for a taxi home.

The effect of this £5 note on GDP would be the same as one person spending £25 in one go. So increasing velocity gives an illusion of more money in the system. As more money chasing finite goods and services means inflation, velocity has a role in creating inflation.

The velocity of money tends to increase more noticeably when poorer sections of a society get new money or when inflation has already started to increase. Poorer people are far more likely to spend any new income immediately and early signs of increased inflation can have the effect of encouraging savers to spend their money to avoid it being devalued.

Increased velocity of money is harder to achieve when we use card payments. This increases short term 'rolling' credit (as in credit cards) but won't necessarily increase velocity, only debt.

## Video 20 - 30 mins

Youtube search - USA's Day Of Reckoning - Hidden Secrets Of Money 7 - Mike Maloney

https://youtu.be/P4_1pwsm5LY

# Inflation as Government Policy

The bank of England's inflation target is a Consumer Price Index (CPI) of 2%. Why is this government policy and will we ever see 2% inflation again? Governments like inflation, it improves the chances of paying down debt. Inflation helps to counter the negative effect that payment of interest has on the money supply.

Albert Einstein, (a clever chap I think we can all agree) said, "Compound interest is the 8th wonder of the world". Compound interest is the effect of the interest becoming part of the capital and then accruing further interest.

At 5% compounding interest £1000 pounds grows

| | |
|---|---|
| year 1 £1050 | (+£50 on £1000) |
| year 2 £1102 | (+£52 on £1050) |
| year 3 £1157 | (+£55 on £1102) |
| year 4 £1215 | (+£58 on £1157) |

Inflation is the other side of that coin. If you have inflation year after year, eventually debts become relatively cheaper to pay down, this could then be the ninth wonder of the world or the antimatter 8th?!

Governments want inflation but why has Mark Carney written so many letters admitting he has failed. There are many forces in play here and now, June 2016.

Inflation has the effect of reducing the value of the money you have over time and it facilitates government's borrowing money to spend now. Inflation is a tax on the population and as mentioned above, the highest 'realistic' levels of inflation/tax are on the poorest, and youngest people in the economy.

It shows the level of arrogance within central banks and governments that they believe they can control these numbers without consequences. I find it hard to believe that the current calm waters will continue for long.

Government policy in favour of inflation/tax has many headwinds to overcome but the only way to avoid a visible default on their debts is to induce inflation. The longer it is missing from the economy, the higher it will need to go to avoid default.

# Quantitative Easing

This is a policy that is used to increase the money supply. Instead of holding an auction to sell the bonds that the government is using to fund its deficit, the Bank of England puts them on their own balance sheet. What started as a government debt is now a B of E debt. The knock on effect of this is that the banks and institutions who were normally buying these bonds at auction, find they have lots more money left at the end of the month.

Not only that, but if the Bank of England cannot meet its quantitative easing target by taking on all newly issued government debt, they will also buy older bonds and other paper assets from the secondary market (from banks and financial institutions). The combination of these actions puts the target level of new money into the system.

### Video 21 - 10 mins - Orwell's Ministry of truth?

Youtube search - Quantitative easing - How it works
https://youtu.be/J9wRq6C2fgo?list=PLslyOrpjJ0z2duArbcMKan_xjl4lt07WW

Always be prepared for lies and diversions from the truth. This Bank of England produced video is typical Orwellian stuff. Notice that when they show money going to homes and businesses they show three of each as if this was the distribution. In fact there should be 80 to 90 houses and just 3 tiny little factories. Only the banks are depicted accurately, massive and overbearing. The commentary also says, "this policy is beginning to work" even though there was absolutely no indication of this when this video was produced and still non today. Always question what you are told, the lies are often hidden in plain sight.

The money that the guilt buying institutions save is left in their capital reserves and can therefore be used to support more fractional lending to the economy. In this way, the B of E hopes to raise the money supply and increase GDP by putting more of that money into the economy. This should boost inflation as well but as we have seen in the last few years, this hasn't worked.

So where has the money gone? This has been decided by the private banks via their debt allocation policies. Average house price increases over the QE period and to date have been around 8.5% per annum (albeit with massive regional disparities). Financial asset prices have gone up as well, both because of the quantity of money coming in has increased faster than the available assets, as well as the possible returns on cash (none) forcing more participants into the market.

Crucially though, micro and SME businesses have struggled to get the funds they need to expand. If a bank lends money to a business, there's a chance it might fail, whereas a house? Well, a house doesn't fail like a business.

Quantitative easing has failed to restore proper growth to the economy. It just boosts asset prices, principally housing and shares but a rich man likes other stuff like art, fine wine, classic cars ohh and while we're at it, perhaps another home by the sea. Sorted.

## Helicopter Money

This exotic policy is a result of a thought experiment by Milton Friedman. He pondered what stimulus would come if the government printed lots of fresh money (actual bills) and dropped it onto the populous from a helicopter. Milton came out against the idea but it's gaining popularity with some economists and politicians who want to stoke up the economy and inflation.

It has been tried before when Japan gave away shopping vouchers during the earlier part of their downturn, it didn't go well. They weren't used in enough numbers to make a real difference and to be effective, they really need to be spent on non imported goods or services. I also read that the Japanese government was considering giving the equivalent of $60,000 to parents of a second and third child. This has not yet been adopted but is a very interesting social engineering/helicopter hybrid and could be an indicator for how this policy may take shape.

I think a 'helicopter money' or what is sometimes now called 'people's QE' policy will be tried in the UK. The question is how will it be implemented and how can a negative effect be avoided by this new money being spent on imports, thus causing a worsening of the trade gap and current account deficit.

I notice that the 'helicopter' debate has shifted a little to cover a lot of scenarios including increased government spending on infrastructure projects. The main differences between quantitative easing and helicopter lending is that QE can be unwound. QE is the Bank of England putting debt onto its balance sheet, debt which may be repaid in the future thus extracting this new money from the economy. Helicopter money is permanent new money. There isn't a distinct mechanism for retrieving it, although the government always has the option of taxing money out of the economy. Helicopter money is mostly untried and that is essentially why it's a very risky course of action.

For instance, If the government chooses to fund the Heathrow expansion through new money creation rather than through guilts or private finance, this will put £20-30 billion into the economy. However, will this really favour just our economy though? As we are still in the EU, governments cannot be seen to favour one EU country over another when awarding contracts like this. Also many of the materials may also be sourced from abroad so we may end up putting substantial amounts of this new money into Germany for trains, China for steel, France for whatever it is they make (I'm still a bit unsure on that). When we are out of the EU, this will be a bit less of an issue but for now, government infrastructure helicopters should be grounded.

# The Bank Bailout

Oh the bailout. I don't want to be a bank or banker basher but they really have no shame. They also have not been punished or regulated in ways that will sufficiently discourage more bad behaviour. Gordon Brown really did let them off the hook and the new governments have let things fester to an extent that there will be a chance to repair the damage sooner than was necessary. I fear another bailout is inevitable unless the powers like neo liberal economists and the IMF are overthrown.

Bailout V.1 – 2008 (Big sequel due in banks near you soon)

We saw Northern Rock go under, it was brought down by the toxic subprime (isn't that a wonderful Orwellian phrase. It's not junk, just *subprime*. I digress) American bank Lehman Brothers was allowed to fail as well. The system was on the verge of collapse, we were told.

Some, not all of British banks were in trouble, they needed cash to survive and the government and the bank of England were the lenders of last resort. The government allocated eight hundred and fifty thousand, million. £850 billion. I think it's worth reflecting sometimes that a billion is a thousand million, This is not a trivial amount of debt money.

The bankers seemed chuffed and went back to business as usual. For example, by 2010 RBS paid out £1.3 billion (yes, billion) in bonuses to some of it's staff after posting an annual loss of £3.6 billion. These super over valued staff had managed to make a massive loss, paid for by their principal shareholder, (the government) and were so miserable about it, they gave themselves massive bonuses to cheer themselves up!

The banks make their money by creating new money out of nothing and charging us rent on it. They also gambled huge amounts of the money (gifted to them by the B of E) as well as the rent from all the new money, on derivatives they didn't understand. When they lost out we gave them yet more money and no one was held to account and banking practices were amended only slightly. It's win, win and win again for them.

The bankers would say, "we pay a lot of taxes and help with the balance of payments". I'm disagree, sort of agree on that and will return to this in the conclusions from this book.

# Derivatives

Much of the global financial crisis of 2007/8 was caused by a problem within the derivatives market, but what are they?

A derivative is a financial product, it's a contract with a provider whose price is 'derived' from an underlying asset like a commodity or company share. There are simple, purely asset based derivatives like ETF's or investment trusts that are consumer facing, and then there are complex derivatives that are for professionals from the financial sector such as hedge funds, banks and insurers.

The derivative contract with a financial company could be as basic as, "we promise you a rate of return the same as the increase/decrease in the price of platinum". In this way you don't actually own the platinum, you own a contract with a company who claim they will match its rate of return.

One of the world's most popular derivatives are ETFs, Exchange Traded Funds. These are funds you can buy that will track a certain index like FTSE100 or the Nasdaq. The price of the ETF is derived from the price of all the shares within that index. This doesn't sound so bad so why all the negative stuff?

Complex derivatives tend to carry more leverage, ie there is more exposure to risk. Imagine you go to a bookmakers and put a bet on a horse, I think the horse is going to be called Gordon Brown. As mad as it seems, you place a £10 bet for it to win at odds of 5 to 1 (leverage). The booky gives you a betting slip. You are now holding a kind of complex derivative. You have a contract with a company, the value of which is derived from the performance of an underlying asset, the horse.

Bookies have innovated lots of different types of bets, each way, accumulators, first goal, all sorts of different bets all related to the performance of underlying assets. Bookies don't call them derivatives but financial companies do and they are even more imaginative. (sorry, as usual Gordon Brown came in last - shame)

When you buy a derivative, you don't own the underlying asset, just a promise related to it. The provider has to decide whether to buy the underlying asset or 'hedge'

If I bought an FTSE 100 tracker ETF, the company selling that to me could take that money and buy the underlying assets so that when I come to sell my ETF, they are covered by the asset value. Guess what, they don't necessarily do that. They will buy a good portion of the assets but they will also sell people onto the other side of that deal. There is an ETF call SUK2 which 'shorts' the FTSE100. This means they are betting for it to go down. This will help to hedge the people who buy the ETF that wants the index to go up. They can also buy derivatives that will hedge the down and upside and they can 'go blind' on a portion which means they have a shortfall on cover of the underlying assets relative to the total value (also known as exposure) of derivatives sold.

The derivatives that caused the 2007-8 crisis were mortgage related products. In the normal process of mortgage lending, a bank lends to the buyer who then uses the money to purchase the house of their dreams. Over time this will reduce the banks ability to keep lending as their capital account is eroded. To free up new money for more lending, the banks were sold the idea of grouping the mortgage debt together into a derivative called a Collateralised Debt Obligation (CDO). The CDO's contained mortgages, car loans and other debt of mixed interest rate and therefore mixed risk. The blended rates offered by the CDO's were very good relative to the yields on other products. The other issue with CDO's was that the ratings agencies all gave them AAA ratings meaning they should never ever go bust, honest. By selling the CDOs, banks effectively cleared their mortgage book. This had the effect of restocking their reserves and they could then find more people to lend to, which eventually drove them towards the 'subprime' market.

The euphoria around CDOs created too much money chasing non productive assets, herding, mania and we all know what happened next. They did go bust, or precisely, the CDO derivatives were packaged in a way that it was very difficult to tell which ones were the ones that would fail. The price of all the CDO's crashed to pretty much nothing. They were toxic. This left banks not knowing which other banks they could trust.

Insurers AIG had insured possible losses believing this was a AAA product. They insured the CDO's with another kind of derivative known as a Credit Default Swap (CDS). These derivatives are used as a risk transfer or hedging mechanism. When the CDO market crashed, banks tried to claim on their hedge insurance derivatives. The exposure to CDOs was so massive, they couldn't pay and this caused the collapse of AIG and its subsequent bail out.

These derivatives were all 'marked to market' which is an accounting practice meaning that if a buyer could be found for the swaps, what would they pay when the market was already collapsing. Unsurprisingly the CDOs were valued at a big fat zero and the CDSs a big, toxically fat zero.

Of course, no significant players were charged or were sent to jail. Many of the key players had a bumper year with seven figure bonuses, so that's nice.

This crash in derivatives had the effect of drastically reducing lending, principally between banks but also to businesses. Therefore the money supply shrank significantly exacerbated by interest payments, and this reduction in money supply caused a recession. This recession cost many jobs and was part of what brought about the gradual reduction in living standards for so many people outside of London.

All complex derivatives should be banned immediately.

The amount of derivatives in circulation is staggering. Deutsche Bank are reported to have over 40 trillion euros worth, many times bigger than the annual GDP of Germany. This is all unrecorded, 'off balance sheet' risk.

For a good example of this 'off balance sheet' principal, consider you are leasing a building worth £2 million and the insurance premium to protect if from fire costs £5000 per year. You may opt to not pay the insurance which improves your profit by £5,000 which will show up on the balance sheet. But the 'off balance sheet' risk is massive. This risk isn't required to be shown on the balance sheet but if your building burns down, you will have to find the £2 million required to rebuild. If your building is also later found to be the cause of a district wide fire however, your liability could be hundreds of millions in third party claims. This event will almost certainly be enough to bankrupt you and your company.

Deutche and all other major banks are at risk of a systemic derivatives crash.

# Gross Domestic Product

This is a measure of the total value of *goods and services* being exchanged within an economy within a given period. We are most often exposed to an annualised GDP growth figure to explain the health of the economy. At the time of writing, the GDP year on year figure is $2.678 trillion (£2.2 trillion) and expected growth a little under 2 percent.

Percentage change of GDP tells us if the economy is growing or shrinking. Governments always hope to have GDP growth but sometimes they fail. A growing economy is required to deal with the debt burden.

Conversely if GDP is negative for two quarters in a row, sorry, you're in recession. During the current, post crisis economy, one of the greatest concerns of politicians and their economic advisers is the threat of recession and possible deflation. Quantitative easing, near zero interest rates and easy lending policies are intended to boost GDP in order to avoid recession. I doubt they will succeed for long.

Forecasting expected growth or contraction is notoriously difficult, but politically significant. Very significant. When you hear an institution making predictions about an economy's future direction, be very wary. This is usually non news. This is the type of news that is not 'new' because it hasn't happened, it's only a prediction of what might happen. By the time the revised and accurate GDP figures are actually announced, normally six months or more later, these non news predictions have been forgotten or forgiven. The institutions know this so they can tweak their prediction to suit their agenda. The IMF kept predicting major gloom for the UK economy while George Osborne was trimming public spending after the 2005 election. More gloom, more gloom, the trouble was, we were doing better than nearly every other EU nation and doing pretty well globally. Economic forecasting is often just political posturing, beware.

Something that doesn't add significantly to GDP is housing. Buying and selling existing houses has little effect on GDP. The exchange of the asset itself doesn't count as nothing has been created, merely the ownership of an existing asset has changed. There is a residual effect on GDP from estate agents and solicitors fees, removal services and DIY, carpets etc. Piffling amounts of money relative to the amount of debt this racks up.

Another thing that doesn't significantly add to GDP is the buying and selling of shares, trusts and derivatives. All that money? Yes, trillions every year traded, not a pimple on the GDP. There is some residual turnover counted within GDP from this activity such as solicitors and support services but a laughably small amount. However, bankers would rightly point out that their sector does massively help with the *balance of payments*.

So two of the largest sectors within the UK unreal economy add little to GDP for all the capital employed. Banks get their money for free (almost), gamble some of it and direct much of the new debt they create into non productive, non GDP sectors. Politicians and economists appear on the TV to say that "we don't know what's wrong, why is the economy not growing? what's wrong with our productivity?", I think they know.

# Goods and Services

Goods and services are the real economy, no, honest, no joke this time. Goods produced in factories or fields and services in offices, studios, shops and restaurants are the backbone of the economy. It's this activity that creates wealth within our communities. Goods and services produced from within the real economy, and by that I would emphasise the private micro and SME sector, also creates the activity that pays most of the new tax income that the other less productive parts of the economy live off.

Micro businesses and small to medium enterprises tend to work in the private sector. They tend to be taxed at a much higher *nominal* rate than large and corporate business. They are however much less likely to retain expensive lawyers and lobbyists to fight for them within government and banking circles.

As I mentioned right at the beginning, the development of new goods and services is an ongoing process whereby they are refined, through experience and our use of descriptive language, to gain a competitive advantage. Our businesses need to be pursuing new markets and sectors to rebuild our economy. With so many innovations in production techniques, materials and delivery, it really is a good time for entrepreneurs to be bringing out new, and refining old products. New materials like GoreTex and Lycra have revolutionised much of the clothing we wear, ski gear for instance is amazing nowadays. To start to rebalance our economy we need far more investment in research into materials to be able to deliver opportunity to UK businesses. We have to bring some manufacturing back to the UK and new products and especially materials, I believe is the way to do that.

Information technology is another area where we need to be playing a bigger role. The UK is doing well in financial technology (FINTECH) but needs to invest and expand when we find a niche where we excel.

Services are harder to make more efficient but not impossible. Artificial intelligence will compete with solicitors and other knowledge based professions and services and robotics and automation will play a bigger role in shops, offices and restaurants.

I believe that the UK should embrace these changes. But without investing in the new businesses we won't be able to make this transition as people will be fearful of losing their current job to a robot, if there are insufficient opportunities to replace them.

# Government spending vs GDP

In 2016 the government spends a whopping £43.2% of total GDP. I would have to say that governments are very bad at spending this much of our money. Nevertheless, the money they spend on the NHS, defence, traffic cones etc does add to GDP. Before the first world war, government spending was around 8.5% of GDP but a couple of wars, the welfare state and increasingly socialist policies of successive governments saw that percentage start to rise and rise.

Government spending, and the taxation and money printing they need to fund it are referred to as the *fiscal* side of the economy.

Government spending as a percentage of GDP got to a level of 50% during the Thatcher years when the UK was going through some major restructuring. Mrs Thatcher took on the large unions, most notably the miners union. This battle and the very poor general economic conditions of the period created a large spike in unemployment, the need for infrastructure spending and the Falklands war coming in the early '80s all added to the problem.

When Gordon Brown was in charge of the Treasury from 1997, government spending as a percentage of GDP began to rise again to a whopping 49.6%. The major difference between this and the previous spike was the general condition of the economy at the time. Mr 'no more boom and bust' managed to spend so much of our money during an up cycle in the economy that the structural change to the public finances would take a generation of determined governments to correct. As you can guess, this means it won't happen.

The trouble with the type of spending that Gordon Brown indulged in is that it was structural, meaning future governments are committed to this spending for a long time. This is mostly why the deficit is still so high and borrowing is still going up (but also for political reasons Osborne ring fenced the budgets of all the big spending government departments). For example public servants now easily out earn people working in the private sector (outside London, which is still most of us 87%), especially when you look at lifetime costs. It's not even close. Many public sector managers and senior officials earn more than the Prime Minister. Some University vice chancellors earn over £400,000. And here's the kicker, this is nothing in comparison to the lifetime cost of these positions. When the incumbent retires on full public sector, index linked, unfunded pension, some other overpaid apparatchik steps into that role. In this way we could, with life expectancy the way it is, end up paying 3, 4 or even 5 people in this positions like this simultaneously! Tony Blair comes in for a lot of stick, quite rightly, but Gordon Brown takes the biscuit when it comes to the shear number of gaffs while in power at 11 and 10 Downing street. (At least he managed not to start a war though!).

I don't like direct government spending. I think the corruption of government, government departments and quangos ensures massive waste. When I say corruption, I don't mean that all government employees are accepting money bribes. Not at all, but there is a corruption inherent in a system trying to cater for so many.

Imagine you can afford a personal shopper. You pay your shopper £40,000 per year to do your shopping, they get to know what you like, food, clothes, shoes, holidays, insurance........ you name it, they'll buy it for you. After a while a friend wants to share your shopper, £20,000 each, great, not quite as good as before but hey ho. Now you share your personal shopper with ten or a hundred, maybe even a thousand people. Do you imagine you still get exactly what you want. Do you think the shopper, with this much work starts buying massive amounts of one type of cereal, one sort of pasta, everyone to Bognor for your hols, everyone gets the same? They are getting offers from suppliers to put their purchasing power with them, not for a lower price necessarily, but maybe there are some other benefits, the supplier makes delivery easier, they make friends and contacts within companies bidding for business, dinners, Wimbledon tickets perhaps. This is how public spending is. The system dictates what you get and the purchasing is inefficient, the system is corrupted due to it's size and the barriers between the recipients of services and those in charge of delivery.

# Fiscal and Monetary

The fiscal side of the economy refers to the government's budget. The government spends money on the NHS, schools, defence etc, as well as debt repayment. They apply taxes to individuals and businesses in order to fund this. Because of the fiscal deficit, the fact that they raise less in taxes than they spend, the government also has to borrow money through the Bank of England to plug the gap. This borrowing adds to the public debt, currently around £1.6 trillion.

All governments try to avoid raising visible taxes. They are unpopular with the people and the politicians like to be liked. This has created a problem with balancing the books because tax receipts are not only reliant on the rate at which a tax is levied, they also require improving incomes and prices to tax. Higher wages, higher corporate profits, higher prices for goods and services (VAT), more drinking and smoking, more petrol and diesel. An increase in these metrics will increase tax receipts without having to make the politically difficult decision to increase the underlying rate. Again, this is a motivation for the government to push GDP and inflation upwards through policy and spending.

The Monetary side of the economy is what the Bank of England controls. Their role is to control the volume of money through the capital accounts of the banks and to set the price of money through the interest rates.

The quantitative easing policy of the B of E is also a monetary rather than purely fiscal policy. If the governments bonds are sold into the market via an auction, this would be a fiscal measure as the money goes directly to government. But QE is designed to free up money in the private banking system so instead of a sale at auction, the guilts are 'bought' by the B of E instead. As there is no actual money, this is often referred to as the B of E putting them 'onto the balance sheet'

Fiscal policy = HM Government tax and spend
Monetary = Bank of England print, loan and rent (interest rates)

Helicopter money could turn into a fusion of the two. If the government chooses to increase the money supply through printing and direct placement into the economy, ie not issuing a bond to the bank of England, this will be a fiscal policy but on the monetary side?! This is how exotic and untried this is.

# Keynes, the IMF and the World Bank

John Maynard Keynes is probably the single most influential economist in the world. He came to prominence during the Great Depression following the bursting of the 1929 stock bubble. His theory is that although markets can be trusted for many things during normal circumstances, market intervention by government would be necessary when facing a slump or depression.

During a depression (deleveraging) people stop spending as much money as they used to as they attempt to pay down debt, or survive being unemployed. This will have the effect of reducing over all demand for goods and services within the economy. Economists call this total demand for goods and services, 'aggregate demand'. As aggregate demand drops their is a contagion effect as the lack of customers reduces income and reduces spending in a downward spiral. For instance, if you no longer get your haircut in a fancy salon but go for the cheapest available or none at all, the fancy salon will have less income and they in turn will have to spend less on wages for instance. This could mean that one of their employees will also have a reduction in spending power and their normal purchases will be affected and so on. (As mentioned earlier, this scenario can also be referred to as a debt deflation spiral, secular stagnation or turning japanese)

This was the problem that Keynes could see and he felt that only governments had the motivation and financial power to halt the downward slump by boosting aggregate demand. This would be done through government spending on anything, how the money was spent was less important than the effect the new money entering the economy will have on boosting aggregate demand so the economy would start to grow.

His ideas were put into practice by President Roosevelt during the 1930's in his massive 'new deal' program of government spending on roads, dams and other projects. This was widely seen as a massive success and helped America to recover from the great Depression.

As a result of this Keynes was very influential during the Second World War and was instrumental in the setting up the structure of international financial governance that was adopted immediately after it. This included the setting up of the world bank and the IMF. These institutions came into being at the Bretton Woods meeting between the great powers towards the end of the war.

I have done a lot of research for this book and have been surprised at what I found out about these two institutions. As the Greeks are finding out, they can be very effective poverty making machines. Many think this is by design but this isn't strictly true. The original purpose of the these institutions has morphed, especially the IMF which today practices exactly the opposite role it was intended for.

The world bank was set up to make loans to developing countries so they can become part of global trade and boost living standards and reducing poverty in underdeveloped countries.

The IMF was set up to give help to countries experiencing crises or depressions. As a country runs out of money they will often need to reduce imports to improve the balance of payments and thus the countries outgoings. This reduction of imports may then cause a downturn in these exporter countries economies also. They in turn may reduce imports, again causing a reaction within their trading partners economies. As this process expands, a whole region of nations can be 'infected' by, what started as just a single country's hard times. Keynes saw that it would be very difficult for a single country to resist the reduction in imports that starts this process. He felt that a supra national body needed to step in and control the contagion effect by boosting aggregate demand as soon as possible. The IMF was set up to boost aggregate demand within the affected countries, support international exchange rates of their currency and to avoid any recession being deeper than necessary and avoid the contagion effect.

Former chief economist at the World Bank Professor Joseph Stiglitz in his book 'Globalisation' says of this role

"As we have noted, Keynes explained why countries might not pursue sufficiently expansionary policies on their own - they would not take into account the benefits it would bring to other counties. That was why the Fund, in it's original conception, was intended to put international pressure on countries to have more expansionary policies than they would choose of their own accord. Today the Fund has reversed course, putting pressure on countries, particularly developing ones, to implement more contractionary policies than these countries would choose of their own accord"

The IMF was intended to put into practice Keynesian economics at an international level while also to give advice and guidance on 'best practice' for running economies in distress. But as Prof Stiglitz points out, the Fund has completely changed direction and now focus on 'austerity' economics while the advice they give is often highly destructive to the nations who follow that advice.

Have these institutions been effective? There is no doubt that they have been useful for some countries, but the evidence is clear that they are now used mostly as instruments of American and now EU foreign policy. The IMF in particular has a negative effect on developing countries as its economic dogma, free markets, has not had the effect that they promote.

In 'Confessions of an Economic Hitman', John Perkins explains how the world bank and the IMF are used to allow American corporations to take control of foreign assets, especially commodities like oil, while creating a heavy debt burden within these developing countries. This reliance on debt then gives America, who control the world bank, leverage over the recipient countries, leverage they use to their national and corporate advantage.

A case in point is the Philippines. The world bank organised a loan for the building of a nuclear power station in Bataan, but as with many world bank loans, little of the money was spent locally. The loan money went straight back to American corporations, in this case, Westinghouse, who's original bid for the power station was $700 million. The final bill was $2.3 billion and that was in 1983 when that was still a lot of money.

However, the completed power station has never been turned on as it shared technology with the 'three mile island' station in America that had a meltdown which occurred during the construction of the Bataan generator. Repayment of this loan took 30 years. So a loan to a sovereign nation is actually a gift to an American 'bid to fail' corporation, at the expense of the populations of extremely poor countries. This, in essence, is part of what the world bank does.

These indebted countries also tend to allow American military bases to be positioned within their borders. America currently has military bases in 140 different countries! The US currently has 5 large military bases in the Philippines where they base their South china sea fleet and response force.

The IMF get involved if the recipient country defaults on their loan repayments or is in financial distress that may lead to a default. Their role is to introduce their 'structural reform package' which involves liberating markets, opening up the country's capital account (which means allowing direct foreign investment - so called 'hot money') and getting control of government spending.

This package of measures is the IMF's default package as it has worked so well for so many years. Not for the countries where it's introduced of course, but for American and now European corporations who can move into these countries, buying up 'distressed assets' and commodities cheap. This is the role that 'vulture funds' have made their own.

The structural reform package is designed to create a recession which is a complete reversal of the original role that the IMF was assigned. Instead of boosting aggregate demand to reduce the depth of a recessionary event and possible contagion, the IMF forces countries to increase interest rates and reduce government spending which has the effect of making the downturn worse, and to last longer than was necessary. By forcing governments to reduce spending under the guise of financial responsibility, the structural reform package creates deflation. On top of this, the IMF insists that countries also open their capital markets and embark on a mass privatisation programme. As we have seen in East Asia, and other recipients of IMF guidance, these reforms will often cause a recession that gives opportunities to US corporations to acquire their businesses and banks at rock bottom prices. In Russia the privatisation programme was so badly botched that it directly lead to the oligarchy state we see today.

As Professor Stiglitz also points out, when things go wrong, the IMF tend to favour western creditors and corporations over the health of the nation. The 'hot' money that enters a newly opened market is often quickly withdrawn when the going gets tough exacerbating the problems further.

"It is understandable then why the IMF and the strategies they foist on countries around the world are greeted with such hostility. The billions of dollars which it provides are used to maintain exchange at unsustainable levels for a short period, during which foreigners and the rich are able to get their money out of the country at more favourable terms (through the open capital markets that the IMF has pushed on these countries). For each ruble, for each rupee, for each cruzeiro, those in the country get more dollars as long as the exchange rates are sustained. The billions too are often used to pay back foreign creditors, even when the debt is private. What had been private liabilities were in effect in many cases nationalised"

As Greece is experiencing now, the economy is unlikely to grow without government spending to boost aggregate demand, but instead they are being forced to cut more spending and 'privatise' public assets. Unemployment is running at around 30% and they are in a cycle that will be very hard to reverse while remaining within the euro. The depth and length of this recession means that it will take many years, probably decades for the economy to recover the lost prosperity.

Although there certainly are things that Greece have got wrong in the running of their economy, the ECB is equally culpable in mismanaging the convergence criteria and the implementation of the single currency. Greece were encouraged by the ECB to increase lending, as were Ireland, Portugal and Spain, while Germany were deleveraging after the decades of reunification costs. Remember, someone has to be in increasing debt to avoid recession and the P.I.G.S were it. A lot of this new money got spent in Germany on cars, and other consumer and capital goods, so it was a big help to the German economy to have this new debt entering the eurozone.

Greece failed to spend enough of the new money they borrowed on capital goods that would have helped them to become more competitive, so they haven't any more ability to repay the loans now than before. They still mostly rely on income from tourism and agricultural exports to earn foreign exchange, which is why Greece are still in a mess and will never repay the IMF.

These various tactics have caused the IMF to be kicked out of south America and most of Africa they are no longer welcome in the far east or

Russia, so their only remaining playground is Europe and a few countries that haven't yet found other donors.

I believe the World bank and IMF's role as international banking organisations is about to change. There are two main changes happening that will trigger the end for the world bank and a change of role for the IMF.

The Asian International Infrastructure Bank is a China sponsored alternative to the world bank. It's role will be the same as the world bank's but the loans will favour Chinese corporations. It remains to be seen if these loans will have the same covert effects as some of those from the world bank. The UK upset relations with America when we signed up to support the AIIB, I'm not sure if we've been forgiven yet.

The BRICS countries (Brasil, Russia, India, China and South Africa) are also creating new financial institutions that will rival the IMF as a bank of last resort as well as starting a competitor to the international clearing system (Swift) run by the Bank of International Settlements (BIS).

The IMF may now be preparing to create the currency of last resort, a world money.

As a footnote, the IMF staff do not pay any income taxes anywhere and are also immune from prosecution for a crime of any sort, anywhere in the world (unless the IMF agree to remove this protection). In the case of former director of the IMF, Dominique Strauss-Kahn who resigned in 2011 over his alleged sexual harassment and rape of chamber maids in his fancy New York hotel. Even if he had raped every chamber maid in the building and had been filmed doing it, he could not have been prosecuted. Like so many other alleged crimes of the elites, they are just allowed to disappear. Would that happen for you or for me? No....the full weight of the law would be felt for sure.

# Special Drawing Rights

The 'money' the IMF uses for international transactions is called special drawing rights (SDR). It's not a currency as such because it doesn't have any notes or coins. It's purpose is to be the unit of account for foreign exchange lending. The foreign exchange reserve accounts of member nations can be backed up by SDRs and they are required to hold a certain level of them. In order to place this SDR money into their economy, recipient countries need to exchange them for a national currency.

The SDR has been made up of a basket of reserve currencies, mostly the dollar and the euro but also include the yen and the pound. Recently the Chinese yuan has been included as well cementing their position at the top table of economic powers.

In his book, 'Death of Money', Jim Rickards postulates that the SDR may have a role as a world currency if the dollar collapse is sufficiently chaotic. Even if the dollar collapse is more managed, there is a major role for the IMF to be the banker of last resort to countries in financial distress as a result. As he points out, they are the only player left with a clean balance sheet, meaning no debt.

# Cryptocurrencies

I really enjoyed learning about cryptocurrencies, principally in Domonic Frisby's book 'Bitcoin'

I personally don't think Bitcoin will be the digital currency that the world will adopt, but it's inventor, mystery man Satoshi Nakamoto has made an amazing contribution to the science of cryptography and probably money. I, like most people, was very suspicious about the idea of a digital currency, but I will try to explain what changed my view.

A digital currency has two main hurdles, double spend and security. Satoshi has offered a technology called blockchain to sort them both out.

The double spend problem comes from the fact that a digital file is easily copied. If a digital file is money, it would be easy to spend it with one person and then spend a copy of the same file with another.

The security problem revolves around the concern over 'hacking', ie the theft of digital files.

Blockchain addresses these issues by decentralising the ledger that records both where the digital money is, and what it has been used for. Every transaction of Bitcoin,(and other crypto's using blockchain technology), is recorded in a digital ledger. Blockchain is the name of the digital ledger which is made from blocks joined together in chronological order. Every ten minutes a new Bitcoin block is created and is a record of all bitcoin activity in that period. The blocks are published and held on individual computers around the world. New bitcoins come into existence when a publisher of the block is chosen by the bitcoin system, via a process known as 'mining'. The block is added to the blockchain ledger and all competing miners update their records automatically.

This process ensures that the transaction ledger is widely held and therefore someone wanting to forge or hack the ledger would need to corrupt data on thousands of different computers almost instantaneously. Therefore, it is secure (ish) and the double spend problem is also solved.

There have been a couple of very large Bitcoin thefts however so there's still a bit of work to do with the vaults. As far as I know, the thefts didn't compromise the blockchain, just the digital vaults where bitcoins were held.

The bitcoin publisher wins the right to publish by solving a mathematical problem set by the bitcoin program. The miners have their computers running constantly, trying to out compute all the other miners to win the new bitcoins produced as a reward. This way of creating new money is called 'proof of work'.

Proof of work is analogous to a miner digging for gold. In the early days of Bitcoin the cost of computing the mathematical problems was very low as there were few miners trying to win the new bitcoins. This is similar to the early days of the gold rush when you could pick nuggets out of the streams and hills relatively easily. As more bitcoin miners joined in, the computers got more powerful, specialised and far more numerous. The cost of mining has therefore gone through the roof as the number of coins has been steadily reduced over time. The rate now is 12 bitcoin for a block after starting at 50.

The miners have spent large sums on computers to increase the speed at which they can solve the mathematical problems set by the Bitcoin software. The speed is known as the 'hash rate'. So just as in the case of gold miners, later bitcoin miners have to dig deeper (more computers) and faster (high hash rate) to earn fewer bitcoin. Bitcoin miners work their computers rather than their shovels as proof of work and I think this does justify the claim of crypto's to having a value akin to money in some ways.

There are many crypto currencies out there, some with slightly different approaches such as Peercoin and Bitgold are of interest to me. Peercoin is based on 'Proof of stake' which means a miner offers a quantity of the peercoin currency, as a bond of good faith, putting your money where your block is. The idea here is that if the miner were to make any mistake in the block, they would lose the bond that they have put up.

Bitgold (now trading as goldmoney) isn't backed by proof of work or stake, it's backed by vaulted gold. This is a very interesting currency option as your deposits are converted into gold and then you can convert your gold into other currencies at a later date. Gold is the classic store of value and could do extremely well against fiat currencies. This has completed the money circle all the way back to the original gold standard.

# Nominal

Metrics like inflation or interest rates sometimes act against, or in combination with each other.

When comparing figures like gross domestic product for instance, the growth (hopefully) needs to be measured in absolute terms which requires the effect of inflation being excluded. This would then be referred to as nominal GDP.

If a country has inflation of 5% and absolute GDP went up by 7%, then the nominal growth in GDP was 2% as 5% of this growth was directly caused by inflation.

The nominal interest rate tells you what the growth has been from increases in productivity, population and trade surplus. The nominal growth allows accurate historical comparison and for this reason it is the number normally used by economists.

When you compare interest rates, investors need to discover the nominal rate to see the true cost/benefits. If you want to save money, the nominal rate is the interest rate you receive minus the rate of inflation.

You need to find the highest rate possible to offset the effect of inflation, which is why a lot of money gets invested in higher interest paying countries like emerging markets. When the dollar or pound interest rate increases, the difference decreases and much of the money invested in emerging markets comes home again for the added safety. This has sparked major problems in emerging markets in the past and could do so again if the US and other major currency rates ever increase.

# Yield

The yield on an investment is the return expressed as a percentage of the cost. So if you pay £1000 for some shares and the dividend paid is £30 per year, the yield is 3%. This is pretty easy but when the shares double in price, the yield stays the same for you as the amount of money you invested hasn't changed but for new investors, the yield will drop to 1.5% (assuming the company continues to pays a £30 dividend).

The yield is inverse to the price. As the price of an asset goes up the yield goes down for people buying this asset.

The yields on government bonds are extremely low or even negative, so if you hold these, you make a low or negative return. Bond prices are in a massive speculative bubble which makes them a waste of money. Insurance companies and banks have to hold these bonds and so they put them into wrappers like trusts and funds in order sell them to us. Most of these assets fail to beat a simple tracker and are not as safe as they made out to be.(IMHO) (DYOR)

Sir Philip Green is getting a lot of grief about the BHS pension, but he wasn't responsible for the pension directly. This has been the case since the Maxwell scandal, the control of a company pension scheme is separated from the company management and handed to trustees. Something that isn't pointed out by the media, except Moneyweek magazine, is that the pension advisors had 81% of the fund invested in bonds. With such low bond yields at the moment, this almost guaranteed that they would lose the battle with inflation and improving life expectancies, thus creating or at least exacerbating the pension deficit.

The role of the central bank is also greatly overlooked. Super low bond yields are policy. Because of this, Mervyn King and Mark Carney are also partly responsible for the BHS deficit, as well as all the other pensions currently in trouble that aren't publicised because they don't have such a watchable bogeyman as Sir Phil.

I'm also sure the advisors of BHS get paid royally for the advice given to the trustees. All these other players have totally avoided public scrutiny of their competence and integrity.

# Conclusions

I hope that this book has given you a better understanding of economics and from reading it, you can see that with a little effort, it should be understandable to most people. In a democracy we definitely should and need to have opinions about it.

When you listen to the news in the future, don't be too surprised if you find that you're being lied to, or at least having your attention distracted by partial truths. I listen to the business news and often to people who either don't understand the nature of money creation and debt, or are playing along with some other agenda. News for the masses, not the classes?

"If you don't read the newspapers you're uninformed, if you do, you're ill informed"

*Denzil Washington.*

I hope that you will also have a view on our ability to create new wealth. Wealth from labour is the surplus created from investment in people, innovation and technology. We used to be brilliant at creating wealth, but we have lost sight of this skill, which there is still a desperate need for.

## Problems

Money. What is the nature of money? Money is debt. Who stands to gain and who controls this debt?

It's been hard for me to become so cynical about our system, but now I have crossed the line and I feel that I can see clearly why the economy isn't working in the way that it should. The real eye opener is that I now also know, in my heart, that this is not an accident. The system we labour

136

under is designed and perpetuated by the real power brokers. Forget democracy…

"Permit me to issue and control the money of a nation, and I care not who makes its laws" Amschel Mayer Rothschild of the Rothschild banking dynasty.

The money is the thing. The debt and the interest are enslaving us and we are willing participants because we haven't seen the downside. We don't see the power, the theft and the risks clearly. I will try, without being overly alarmist, to describe the nature of the system, the matrix.

The financialisation of our economy and of us, through debt creation, is built into our system and without a doubt, is fully understood by the people in charge. The big three; the banks, the government and the corporate interests, control and run the economy to their advantage. Democratic intervention is almost impossible when the huge majority of people, including many politicians, don't understand what's going on.

The banks start to take control - There was an interesting occurrence in New York in 1975. The city wanted to issue more bonds to the banks through what had been until that day, a routine auction. On this day however, the banks simply didn't show up. The banks decided they would not make any further loans to this debt laden city without the city agreeing to some new rules. The banks said "no representation, no money" and demanded the right to intervene in putting the city finances back on track. The next committee to run the city finances had eight bankers and just one elected representative from the city board. This is, in essence, how most countries are now run. Not quite so overtly as then, of course, but Governments still need the banks to fund their over spending, so the banks always get their interests prioritised.

The situation in most central banks around the world has got to such a state where much, if not all, the current national debts will go unpaid. America will never manage to pay it's debts, never. It's an impossible task. At some point they will default and at that time, inevitably, almost every other nation will default as well. The only question is, how long will it be?

The debt burden. Compounding interest makes it impossible for a indebted country to repay as their debt approaches or exceeds 100% of GDP. Developed nations have struggled in recent decades to get growth back to the long term norm of 3%, however our total private and public debt burden will be compounding faster than this and as a result we will never be able to repay, we will only continue to build the debt until the day the fan gets congested.

Why would the banks and our government allow this to happen? The reason, I suspect, is that there's very little downside for the banks in particular and the government are clearly gutless frauds. The current system allows the banks, the bankers and those in the financial industries to access lots of cheap money with which they can buy assets. The people who get the new money first get a chance to spend it before the inflationary effects of new money reduce its' spending power. The further away you are from new money, both geographically and socio-economically, the worse off you are when you finally see some of it. This new money will have been devalued in itself and will also have the effect of devaluing the money you already had, like your salaries and savings.

The banksters will own so many properties, businesses, gold, fine art, classic cars and other resources that any reset, while temporarily inconvenient for them, will not change their position in the pecking order.

When the system does implode or reset, the banks will be bailed out again and still be put in charge of the new money system, so as always, they will get the new money first and will be able, as now, to use it at full value before inflation inevitably reduces its' purchasing power.

The new money system will probably be designed or overseen by the IMF, fundamentally a lobby group for the banks, which will put central bank governors firmly in charge of getting their countries finances restarted. The banking system will thus be perpetuated and the political power of banks, already huge, will be increased even further.

The banking system. We have an independent central bank that acts as an intermediary between the government and the private banks and financial organisations. Now, more than ever, the central banks around the world are using monetary policy to promote the interests of private banks. Quantitative easing has fuelled the financial divisions in countries where it has been tried. Perhaps this is what the bank of England video meant when they said that 'there were signs that the policy was working'? Not working for the general economy, but working to make the banks rich.

The banks are offshoring profits both at a corporate level and as individual bankers for their rich clients. The banks facilitate and exploit these tax havens to the detriment of the worker bees who have no alternative but to pay their due taxes. Despite the bailouts, the banks are continuing to be complicit in the depletion of the tax income of the government and thus, its' ability to fund proper investment (if they were bothered!).

The bailouts continue. There is such a massive mismatch between the way individuals are treated and the way banks and corporates are treated when they get into financial difficulty. The banks know that poorer people are generally honest. Individuals tend to believe that a debt is a debt and it's their duty to repay it. People with payday loans and credit card debts make huge profits for the banks and these people are continually offered more and more credit until it becomes unmanageable and then they are fined and hounded to pay the interest, keep paying the interest, keep paying. This isn't the case with the banks and corporates who tend to default or, as they prefer to call it, "restructure their borrowing". And this happens all the time, if the low cost loans of the big boys are still a bit too high, just restructure again. Even better, they could persuade the government or customers to bail them out. We, the worker bees, are always bailing industries out, but not the little ones of course (no lobbyists), just the big uns. They sometimes call the bailouts subsidies or grants, inducements or enterprise schemes. Very creative!

The level of corruption is massive. Remember the scheme where students had to go to work for an employer for no pay? No pay at all just so they can gain 'experience'. Guess who the chosen employers for the free labour were? Only the big corporates and the government themselves were the lucky recipients of this gift. Fortunately, this was successfully challenged and stopped.

Digital money. The move towards digital money by using contactless payments will also fuel a greater level of debt amongst the younger consumer. The credit card companies and retailers know that people will tend to spend much more when using a card payment than if they pay by cash and therefore they are motivated to continue to try to increase their use.

There is a phenomenon known as 'the pain of payment' which describes why we experience a strong, negative emotional response when paying in cash. There is an immediacy to a cash payment that creates a feeling of loss, which has the effect of inhibiting our spending. When using credit cards as an alternative to cash, and especially with contactless, we don't get the same feeling of loss and consequently we spend more. Who is most likely to use contactless? Probably debt laden students. As the limit on contactless payment, which is £30 currently increases, I suspect we are going to see even more credit card debt problems.

Debt slavery. Ordinary workers in private businesses are now more reliant on their jobs because of the debt they have all taken on in order to live. Repayments have to be made and this reduces the workers' willingness to put their current employment at risk by asking for better pay. The massive influx of well educated and motivated workers from Europe and elsewhere has also had the effect of anchoring wages down towards the minimum wage. It's getting harder all the time for ordinary workers to find a job in a private business that pays much above this minimum. This will continue to depress wage growth. (I emphasise private business because this is the area where the real wealth is created and real taxes are paid.)

The tax hole. The banks, lawyers and accountants who run the tax avoidance schemes and offshore their profits are simply taking advantage of the government's inability to write decent new laws. Why doesn't a government reform the laws and put an end to this? They appear to have no incentive to do so but I cannot understand why. The effect is that a vast sum, (according to HRMC's own estimates it is around £36 billion per year) is going uncollected. This sort of money would go a long way to sorting out our balance of payments. Why don't they do it?

If businesses incorporated in the UK, such as Facebook, Amazon or Starbucks, who claim they don't make any money and therefore don't want to pay their fair rate of tax, then they should not be operating in this country at all. The fact that the corporate sector is holding billions of pounds worldwide in offshore tax havens to avoid having to pay tax on it is a massive distortion to business motives. They are not reinvesting in their own businesses or the infrastructure of their host countries. The corporates are getting as rich as some of the richest countries in the world.

Government employees don't pay tax. The people working directly on government contracts don't pay tax in effect, the unemployed don't pay tax, and many people who are employed and earning middle incomes effectively don't pay tax either because of the tax credit system. The upper limit for universal credit is £23,000 per year, which is the equivalent of a non government job that pays around £33,000 (without any tax credits). Many corporates also pay no tax and many pay extremely little tax, when you deduct the tax credits that the government pays out to their employees. So who the hell is left paying all the tax?

The deficit is not a surprise when you consider that so few people actually contribute to the treasury. We are led to believe that some of the above groups do pay in, but they actually don't. If you are paid by the government directly, or as a contractor, then you do not contribute to the tax income. The people in 11 Downing street know this, so why are they not taking some action?

And there are the other taxes. Regulation has become a massive industry. I am not against regulations necessarily, but the level and types of regulation imposed on small and medium business is far too high and the cost of 'enforcement' is unjustifiable. Ticking boxes and doing reports doesn't make a business better, it certainly doesn't identify the poor business practices, just the lack of good paperwork. Health and safety, food standards, product standards and so on are designed to create jobs within the compliance industry and this is the real reason for these regulations. Do you believe that an ever expanding compliance industry will improve business in general? I certainly don't. Compliance is a tax on small and medium businesses and helps to create barriers to expansion and competition. Regulations have had the effect of making UK businesses uncompetitive, so now we buy massive amounts of consumer goods from other countries who have little or no regulation.

My own industry, dentistry, has seen a huge number of new regulations introduced, which are changing the way we do business. I am a dental technician, but I do not actually have any formal qualifications. I am certainly not saying that this is ideal, but the imposition of a degree level for entry onto the technician register (after I "qualified" via a grandfather clause) has imposed a massive tax on our business. I suspect that as a result of this, our industry will dwindle down to a pretty small number of technicians, but with more and more machines.

Technicians have escaped the worst of the compliance regulations, but the surgery side of the industry has received a barrage of regulations, which has had the effect of making some space for the corporates to enter the market, because many former principles (practice owners) no longer want to deal with all that paperwork. Compliance is something that the corporates have whole departments specifically set up to deal with. This means that surgeries will be run more and more by a few large corporate interests, who will push down on external costs (dental technicians - ouch!) whilst trying to manage their internal costs and increase their profits. Will all this compliance and a move towards the corporate provision of dentistry push up standards? Time will tell, but I very much doubt it.

Compliance is generally a tax on innovation and competition as smaller businesses struggle to put enough time into the paperwork that has no immediate effect on good employers, but the bad ones can tick some boxes, knowing that this will be enough to keep inspectors happy. It's also rather sad that the people who work in the compliance industry often seem to earn far more than productive workers. Some years ago the position of 'Hand hygiene officer' was advertised with a salary of around £70,000 per annum!!!? Can this be right? The rent seekers are a tax.

Financialisation. Our stock market system is badly broken and it is a fraudulent, self serving exercise. Share trading, to a very large extent, is yet another tax. Shares are so often traded for the sake of the trade itself, because every trade creates a fee for the brokers. High speed trading has no real purpose within the market at all. The use of mega fast computers to trade billions of shares, hundreds and thousands of times, is robbery. This is a tax on wealth, our wealth. The financial wizards are not making money, they are taking money, and this needs to be stopped. Unlike visibly competitive businesses, finance has a high level of cartel like operation and the full weight of government protection to ensure their survival, no matter how poor their performance. I would say that the finance industry taxes us and then gives government a cut for their protection. Cut out most of the middlemen and that tax will disappear.

Inflation. This is actually government policy. By inflating the amount of currency within the economy, the Government are actually debasing its' value. Any wealth that is created is constantly being eroded through inflation and with interest rates near zero, there is no safe place to get protection. The Government would like to erode the value of the debt by diminishing its nominal value, and this action steals from savers and from wealth accumulated within pensions, as well as creating price inflation in the areas that this new money turns up, such as housing and shares.

Through these various mechanisms; money printing, bank control, debt slavery, under taxing, government spending, regulations on private business, poor regulation on the financial industry and inflation, the government is allowing a system to survive that shifts more and more wealth from the people who have little of it, on to those who already have a lot. Any government that is not corrupted could change many of these structures very quickly. Some changes, like controlling government spending take far more time, but they could be done.

## Why are the rich getting richer while the poor are growing in numbers?

First, a definition of 'rich' and 'poor' as these words can be misinterpreted very easily and I want to make sure that these words reflect my conclusions.

'Rich' people own more than 50% equity in their homes and have a household income above £40,000 after tax putting them in the top 10% of incomes.

'Poor' people rent their home and have a household income of less than the median income of around £30,000 before tax.

Here it is then, the reasons are actually quite simple in my opinion. There are four main reasons why this is happening and will continue to happen while the money and tax system remain as they are.

1. Younger worker bees are not living within the Bank of England's world of 1% inflation. The CPI figure is corrupt and only suits the baby boomers and the rich. The increase in the price of housing is real inflation affecting younger families and individuals and means that for them, nominal growth has been negative for years. (If absolute growth is 2% but inflation for young worker bees is 4.5% when you account for housing costs honestly, then nominal growth is in effect -2.5%). These people are in a debt deflationary spiral where housing costs completely dominate monthly expenditure because rents and house prices increase much faster than the CPI figure.

2. We are all on benefits now but the rich get more than the poor. Since buying our commercial property in 2010, the value of our home and commercial together has increased by around £200,000. As this increase is almost entirely due to the monetary policies of the B of E and the government, you can, and I think should, see this as a benefit. The more expensive the house (nearer London) the more you generally get. In our case that is around £28,500 per year between us in state 'benefits' which could easily have the effect of refunding any tax we pay. The trick is this payment is deferred so we don't see it as the injustice it truly is.

   The way that money is gifted to people who already own assets massively disadvantages those who don't. As rents broadly run in line with house values, renters are double paying. They pay for increased rents and also, effectively pay for the 'perk' of the landlords house price inflation as mentioned above. This effect means people who own assets will continue to build wealth broadly at the expense of those who do not. (Technically, this is a monetary inflation problem, those who own assets avoid it while those that don't have their wages, savings and future downgraded).

3. The failure of the tax system to establish a fair distribution of the tax burden has left the richer people in our society, i.e. those who have capital, relatively under taxed in comparison to those who rely solely only on their labour for income. Without taxing capital, like government gifted capital gains in the housing market, these gaps will continue to grow and further entrench the haves and the have not's in our society. Social mobility is currently at a very low level in the UK suggesting, not only that this isn't changing, but that it will continue to get harder and harder to get on.

4. Although net migration to the UK has a very positive effect on our demographics and skills base, this has also increased competition for jobs, which inevitably leads to a suppression of wages. This effect, coupled with the moves towards automation, CAD/CAM and robotics greatly reducing the role of the skilled labourer, means that wages are likely to be more rooted to the minimum

wage set by government, and they are beholden to big business, not worker bees.

## Solutions?

I believe that as a country without many natural resources that could create wealth for us, we have to invest in our population. As a first world country we have a well developed education system, which gives us a massive advantage over human capital in the much of the rest of the world. However, our educators have let us down for several generations and we cannot afford to continue to slip backwards in international education league tables.

Teachers seem to fear academic success of the few as they see this as a cost to the many. This is a retarded attitude which needs to be set aside so that we can invest properly in our most academic talents. Not exclusively, of course, but the most intelligent students require 'special needs' attention at least as much as those at the bottom, who are currently the only ones classed as 'special needs'.

Holding back the brightest doesn't improve the education of the majority. Indeed it has quite plainly failed to do so as by international standards, our children are falling further back every year while the establishment tell them they are getting brighter.

I don't blame individual teachers for this, they are good, honest and committed people, but the system and attitudes of teacher training, their unions and the educational establishment are all wrong. A two tier system, while not enough tiers in my opinion, is good and inevitable, not bad. Life is many tiered. Teachers themselves wholly endorse a two tier system in schools of course - when it comes to their pay. Do they insist that the cleaners and dinner staff are paid the same as them, do they moan and wrench with grief that they have such an advantage in pay and conditions?

I would say at this point that the teenagers emerging from our schools appear to be much more mature and 'rounded' individuals than before, and this is clearly a very positive thing.

I'm sure feathers will have been ruffled and there is some bristling and tut' tutting going on out there. Sorry. Policy should be based on facts and results. The fact that we are throwing away our educational system on the premise of 'equality' is shown in the results. Not the fantasy league table provided by our department of education, but how we are doing relative to the competition. According to the OECD, we are still just in the top 20 in the world for educational achievement up to the age of 15. If we don't do something to improve our system soon, I suspect we will be overtaken by more ambitious and pragmatic countries very soon.

Higher education also needs to be looked at more realistically. Many students are leaving university with useless degrees and lots of debt, I can't see how that's a good start in life. If everyone has a degree, then this is no longer a differentiator which makes the value of many degrees extremely limited.

Conversely, Switzerland is one of the very top countries for income, quality of life, educational standards and wealth creation. It's a heavily industrialised country that would make a very good model for our own economy. They also have one of the lowest rates of degree level education amongst OECD countries. Less than 20% of the Swiss population acquire a degree.

Now that exam results are treated as absolute rather than relative, the education establishment is easily able to 'cook the books' and this cheats nearly everyone out of what they deserve. It used to be the case that only the top 5-7% of students sitting an exam would get an A or a first. It's quite possible that soon, everyone will get the top mark as it can be set anywhere that suits the establishment. If you only need a 20% mark for an 'A', pretty much everyone will get top marks making it a worthless exercise. Graduates from England and Wales last year achieved a new record pass rate with a quarter of students achieving a first. 75% of all students got a 2:1 or better. How can employers use this information?

I think everyone should have the chance to study a degree level course, but the costs to the student should reflect the usefulness of the degree to the economy. Why are engineering students having to pay for their education? Mathematicians, scientists, teachers and doctors? The country should fund those students who choose to study the trades that we need for social reasons, like doctors and teachers, and those that we need for wealth creation like engineers.

Many of the educational establishment will say that the people who are not selected for the highest academic education are 'thrown on the scrapheap'. Even if this were partly true, there is no need for it to be so. Massive Open Online Courses (MOOCs) give a fantastic opportunity for lifelong learning.

These are outside of the control of the educational establishment, so they are not promoted, but they are flexible, part time courses run and adjudicated by some of the best universities in the world.

I believe MOOCs can give people who choose not to go to university for whatever reason or motivation, an opportunity to pick up their education at a time more suitable for them.

I was a late developer and a typical boy; more interested in mucking about, girls, and trying to look 'cool' than my education. I scraped through some A levels, did one year at university and then dropped out. Academia was not for me, it seemed, and I ended up working in my father's business as a dental technician.

This was an apprenticeship course at the time, but with an appropriate MOOC, I could have gone on to get a degree, which is a requirement to be the owner of a dental laboratory in Germany, and it would be sensible if it were the same here. But as with so many other vocations, the powers that be have made a degree the entry level for dental technology. How utterly ridiculous. As with nursing (soon policing) and other vocations that have turned into professions, many people who could make very good dental technicians will no longer come into this business. Why weigh yourself down with £44,000 of debt, just to become a low paid artisan? The massive open online courses would be a far better route for the more talented within these roles to set themselves apart and build their careers.

Tax policy is upside down as it favours the large company over small and startup companies. These competitors should have all the tax advantages on their side. If we don't have new, innovative business models being tried out by the market, our big players will sit and fester. Small competitive businesses need to have time to get some experience and market share. Yes, many of them will fail, but only through failure in the market will you find the successes.

I think small businesses should have at least 3 years without having to pay any tax, not even employers contributions or VAT. Of course there would need to be rules to stop them closing and re-opening after three years, but again, two sides of text and honest accounting practice should do it.

We should be prosecuting the accountants more often. They get away with far too much and oversee each other's work. This is corrupt practice.

Small innovative businesses are the lifeblood of our future, but now they tend to be targets for the non tax paying, cash rich corporates. Apple, Facebook and Google (Alphabet) are now 'technology plays' meaning that they have bought so many emerging tech companies that their value is far wider than their core business.

## Is this a problem?

Damn right. At the turn of the 19th century, world markets were dominated by railway companies. By mid century, oil and then telecoms companies had come to the fore. Now, oil, pharmaceuticals and tech dominate. If the tax free money of the big corporates hoovers up emerging companies, the public will be unable to invest in these new technologies, except via one of the aforementioned giants. These giants don't want to pay the profits back to the shareholders in dividends, which is the real wealth they earn. But if we don't invest in Google and the like, we will be left with the equivalent of railway stocks.

The unfairly acquired offshore cash deposits of the multinationals need to be taxed and then invested in their businesses or paid to the shareholders in dividends. Regulators like the monopolies commission need to wake up and prevent the formation of monopolies. (Regulators are really crap at doing their jobs.)

Our share based economy is not healthy either and it is not investing in wealth creation sufficiently. Our larger companies that have shares in their businesses sold into publicly traded ownership are not creating good long term results. This is largely because the 'owners' of these listed companies are the least invested stakeholders. If you work in the business, supply the business with services or sub contract work, you really want the business to do well. Paradoxically, if you own shares in the business, you may not care a jot how successful the business is. 'Investors' (speculators) may only be looking for how the share price performs on that day, week or month. High speed trading algorithms only see ones and zeros, not people and plant, they don't trade on the 'value' or success of the companies. Senior management in these businesses also seem to be paid huge amounts, no matter how badly the business does.

Companies should not be allowed to borrow money to pay a dividend. This practice is a distortion of accounting and accountability. Only companies that actually make money should be able to pay dividends.

We need to change the way the shares of our listed companies are traded. Buying and selling a share of ownership is not an end in itself. It was intended as a way of business raising money for expansion and investment and this should again be the focus. Trading shares does relatively little for GDP but if the companies spent more time on actually growing the core business rather than prioritising the share price, we may see some real growth and wealth creation.

A company selling shares has the price locked in at the time they sell them into the market. In the same way as if you sell an asset like a car or house, you shouldn't need to care what it sells for later, you already have the proceeds of the sale. The same should largely be true for a company if the aim of selling shares is to raise money for investment.

I would like to see short term share dealing treated very differently to long term investing. The best way to do this is with the tax system. Taxation on capital gains should be brought in line with that on labour, but one way to encourage a longer term approach to investing would be to offer a tax break for people and investment companies who hold UK listed shares for more than three or maybe five years. I believe this will encourage more people into small retail investing and give firms a reason to look beyond just the next couple of quarters results.

Professor Steve Keen has put forward an interesting proposal on amending the way shares are traded. His idea would be to create a new class of share that had a limit on the number of times it can be traded. He suggests 7 trades. On top of this, after the seventh trade, the share would also have a life limited to a set period, he suggests 50 years, before it expires. This will obviously help to discourage speculative trading and ensure investors are concentrating on the business fundamentals and profitability.

I would also like to see the end of short selling, high speed trading and all derivatives except index trackers, the rules of which can be written in a couple of lines of text. These are distorting factors in the market as they aren't a reflection of what the stock market is for. The stock market is there to allow productive companies to raise money directly from investors to fund expansions and new technologies and we need to get back to this principal.

The total amount of traded assets like derivatives, shares, precious metals and commodities is far, far greater than the total wealth of the world economy. Madness?!

Financial traders make money on volatile markets, it's in their interest to see constant fluctuation in share prices. Short term traders upset the market and make it harder for investors looking at long term gains to stay in the market. Trading costs are a big drag on a portfolio, but fear and greed created by turbulent markets make it harder for amateur investors to stay invested. This 'over trading' tends to lead to underperformance which drives most people into the arms of the 'professionals'. The professionals are an even bigger drag. Most professionals don't beat the market, they have no alpha. Professionals are a tax on worker bee wealth, but if you can find a fund with good alpha (a measure of how much they beat the market index by) then they are worth the money. Good luck with that.

The country's balance of payments also needs to be addressed. We can't run a permanent trade account deficit as we will eventually run out of things like large corporations to sell, and may not be able to bring sufficient inward capital investment to plug this gap. I believe this is a big, BIG problem.

The only way to bring wealth back to the UK, for all, is to rebuild our manufacturing, IT, science and technology sectors. People working together to create a surplus, real wealth. To make that happen we need government policies changed, far better schooling and training as well as supportive banks, stock market and infrastructure spending. We also need to see the financial sector as a function of, and servant to, wealth creation, not as wealth itself.

## The future

The UK economy certainly faces a lot of challenges. We will struggle to implement effective change to our own situation and we are powerless to affect the dismal state of other economies like China, much of Europe and the USA. The world is now very interrelated internationally, more so than ever before.

Is the world economy totally buggered then? Well, my opinion is not yet, but there are many new problems to overcome, as well as all the usual suspects brought on by the debt cycle. If a chaotic crisis is to be avoided we will need strong political leadership and a generation to sort out our debts.

I think there's little doubt that America, and especially the dollar will have to stand aside from their position of dominance in world trade. The amount of dollar debt that is currently supported by the petrodollar system will have to be unwound at some point and it seems unlikely that an American president of either party can make this happen. The debt ceiling has only gone one way and will continue to be expanded as American's are grossly under taxed, or more honestly, the US government grossly over spends. The likelihood then is that a major event will create a collapse of the dollar. The rest of the world will be powerless to prevent the fall out.

China hold masses of American debt and could quite easily use this as a political weapon, for instance if the conflict in the South China Sea starts to get hot. China dumping dollar debt and oil producing countries trading outside the petrodollar as the BRICS and others are planning, will certainly cause the dollar to fall considerably, as well as causing inflation in America as excess dollars come home. This will hurt China as well, but they have the foreign reserves to fight this battle and are less accountable to their population.

One of the new things we are facing is the way that the global market has found a fairly common cycle amongst the developed nations. The financial crisis of 2008 seems to have brought the major countries in line which means that we grow together and we will contract together. All major countries contracting at the same time is not going to be good. We haven't seen that since the 1930's when the last major financial reset happened. I for one, hope that this scenario can be avoided.

As for the UK, we certainly have a lot of problems, the economy isn't as strong as it could be due to the levels of debt created in the last 30 years. Far too much of that debt has been channelled into unproductive and speculative investments, especially in housing and land.

There is no doubt in my mind that we need to change the banking structure from the top down. If I had an independent person running my personal and business accounts, I would be very concerned about my future. Can I trust this person to make sure I have enough money, that the mortgage is paid, that they don't start gambling with MY money. In short, I would sack Mark Carney today and not replace him. He's been smug and wrong in equal measure. His record of forward guidance was a disaster, his QE policy is very questionable and he has grossly misled people with his ridiculous comments pre brexit.

The Bank of England should be brought back into the control of the Treasury so we can have political accountability for the monetary policy rather than trusting ex Goldman Sachs executives whose records around the world do not inspire any confidence of integrity, honesty or competence.

The amount of money in the economy is so crucial that this should be at the heart of our economic strategy. This is a political and democratic issue and I think we need a solution that has as much oversight as possible, but ultimately I believe this needs to be in the hands of our government.

I would strengthen the monetary policy committee by broadening the membership to include non specialists and representatives from productive industries and commerce. I would then hand interest rate policy to them. There would need to be a mechanism for the Chancellor to override in some circumstances but only in quite extreme situations. A chancellor overriding the MPC recommended rate would have to justify themselves to the public and parliament.

The private banks need to be much more highly regulated to prevent them from using their preferred lending allocations to pump up asset prices. They have been granted the gift of money creation, but I believe our government should now put limits on the amounts and direction of the new loans issued.

The banks certainly needed to be rescued in 2008. We would have taken an enormous risk letting more banks fail, but what was Gordon Brown doing giving them all that money without a single concession or prosecution? Never again.

Currently around 80% of new credit goes into the housing sector, this has driven up house prices and led to a situation where they are valued as investments as much as a place to live. Younger people can't even get started now as the average age of a first time buyer reaches 36, in London it's 40. Rents also keep going up to reflect the higher capital cost of the properties.

With my proposed 15% tax on capital gain and a limit of 40% of new loans going to housing, the steam will be taken out of this market. House prices could start to fall quite dramatically and find a 'fair' market value. These measures will put a lot of people into negative equity if there is no debt write down.

I think there should be a partial, one off debt write down, i.e. helicopter money or debt jubilee. And then, new debt has to be limited. People's ability to get new loans has to be reduced and limited to a percentage of their total income. This can only happen if the overall debt burden is going down relative to wages.

The banks must be forced to support productive industries, they currently only allocate 3% of new loans to business and this is nowhere near enough. The postwar Japanese system of window guidance where banks were told how much credit, and to which industry sectors it should be allocated may be a bit much, but what we have isn't working and I think some legislation will be necessary if banks don't start lending sensibly to entrepreneurs and growing SMEs voluntarily.

The banks won't make the profits they have been used to as the rate at which businesses fail will be relatively high, but remember, they created the money from nothing so they lose nothing when loans go bad. Perhaps banks that are bad at lending money should be allowed to go out of business, just like any other enterprise that fails in a competitive environment.

A new breed of bank needs to be created that fulfills the role of high street banks of today. They can create new money with loans, mortgages and credit cards, as well as administering transactions between customers. Retail bank customers currently have a bank guarantee, from the government, insuring deposits up to a defined maximum. This is currently £85,000 but no one needs that much money for 'on demand' deposits but if they do, I suggest they are wealthy enough to pay for insurance themselves.

The £85,000 government guarantee on deposits is a classic 'moral hazard' giving banks no real need to take their depositors money seriously. After all, they and their customers will all get bailed out if they go bust. If individual depositors had to insure their cash as you would your home, a market for this insurance will signal any increased risks associated with individual banks. Insurance for risky banks would become more expensive in the same way as home insurance is more expensive when you have a flood risk. You have the option to pay the insurer, find cheaper insurance or MOVE. This is easier with a bank account than a home but this may, and should have the effect of customers moving to the safer banks and at the same time improve the behaviour of the bankers themselves.

If banks go bust, we should welcome this, claim on our insurance and go and find a safer bank. I would suggest that this insurance cost will only affect the richer within society and it is fair that they should pay to insure their own money rather than the burden falling on everyone. This government guarantee should be cut to twice the monthly median salary, This would make it around £4,750 at the moment.

Any deposits greater than the new guarantee scheme £4750 limit can be insured by the depositor or any uninsured cash reserves over this would need to be diverted out of the retail banking sector and into bonds, shares or newly created 'savings and loans' institutions.

'Savings and loans' would be like building societies used to be. They take depositors money and lend it out, at interest, which is paid to the depositor minus costs. They would not have the power of money creation. They would be non profit societies set up by non banking institutions like pension funds, insurance funds, trade unions or other accountable bodies. I would, for instance, see savings and loans putting investment into houses or housing associations (30%), and (70%) into government and private infrastructure projects, corporate bonds and UK shares.

With savings and loans institutions we can create a savings culture that is actually backed by something. Money backed by the wealth and infrastructure of our own nation. I see 'Savings and Loans' as being more like sovereign funds, developing a country and giving an incentive to save.

One infrastructure project these funds could be directed to is a mass rebuilding of high quality housing for rent. Low cost, secure and controlled rent to allow younger workers especially to get decent housing and have some security of tenure. Savings and loans could fund housing associations and councils wanting to provide these homes.

I believe we should be building prefabricated houses to the best possible specification and then renting them out to working families and individuals for very low rents. If you are paying only three to four hundred pounds a month to rent a zero carbon, self sufficient home, think of the opportunity this would be. Less stressful, happier and healthier lives perhaps.

Over time we could knock down millions of inefficient homes and replace them with new prefabs for sale or for rent. Replacing the housing stock is one of the few ways we can achieve long term reductions in carbon dioxide emissions and free people from debt slavery.

The private sector generally needs more competition and less regulation. Not all regulation is bad, we get used to quite a lot, but regulation has become an industry who feel that employers have to prove their innocence, rather than a branch that investigates reports of poor practice. Ticking endless boxes does not make someone a good or bad employer.

Most of our European competitors haven't got 'gold plated' regulations, they don't have endless 'elf and safety, competing environmental agencies, they don't need to constantly fill in forms to prove they've done something. We need to get this under control.

The larger businesses lobby for and welcome regulations as they can easily afford to have whole departments dedicated to compliance. These regulations unfairly hamper smaller competitors which stifles competition and innovation.

Instead we need proper sanctions for companies who abuse their staff, make dangerous products, pollute the environment or act in other ways that fair legislation has prohibited. Fines should be proportional to the crime and the size of the business involved.

Britain has a fantastic opportunity at the moment to revise our economy and position in the world during our Brexit phase. My proposals of having banks, government and educators concentrating more on business will help, but we will need much more to successfully rebalance towards manufacturing and science. The banks will be slow to put money into business unless they are pushed and houses won't be driving credit creation as they have in the past. We need to boost the productive parts of the economy to boost GDP and grow ourselves out of the debt burden.

As much as it pains me to say it, to avoid a long term recession, the government will have to continue to spend, or allocate funds at or above the current rate of 43% of GDP. To avoid a recession we will need new money to be pumped into the economy because of the underlying debt burden. That will be quite a task and will require loads of luck and strong leadership.

Government spending needs to be reorganised so that any stimulus is temporary, and the on and off balance sheet debts are lowered. The only way, that I can see, for a government to maintain or increase short term spending but reduce long term debts and liabilities is to privatise as much of its spending as possible.

When a government takes on the role of employer, the debts will increase as the government is generally a very generous employer, too generous I would say, it doesn't tend to downsize later, and it's a very inefficient spender.

Privatisation needs a rethink to avoid the corruption and 'bid to fail' mentality of the big firms and to deliver value for money. I would like to see a limit on the size of contracts given to any corporation and an upper limit on the percentage of income derived from government contracts by private firms. In

2012-13 for instance, over half of Serco's UK income was from the government. I think this is too much and can lead to scandals like the dead prisoner tagging. If government contracts could form no more than 20% of any firm's business and at least 30% of these contracts are awarded to firms valued at less than £50 million and 20% to firms valued at less than £5 million, this could produce a far more competitive environment which is more likely to deliver value for money.

Value for money is very important, and a rarity in government spending, but the real bonus is that privatising as much spending as possible removes the long term burden of paying for government worker pensions. That is how the long term debt can be reduced while maintaining short term spending.

There are loads of things a brave and lobby resistant government could do right now to boost the economy.

Build the bloody airport already, I don't care which one. Get it done. (I secretly suspect this rant will still be 'good to go' if you're reading this book in 2030)

Nuclear power, lots of it. The government wants a new Trident submarine, why don't we build lots of them? At a billion pounds a piece we can have four submarines as planned to carry the nukes, and then keep building them as micro generators. They have an outstanding safety record, you have built in redundancy as one going down for maintenance won't scupper the whole network. They can be harboured all round our coastline in existing ports. The generator version could be smaller or have two or more nuclear power plants on for increased capacity. All we will need is some underground capacity to carry the electricity to the existing network.

If we can design and build a fantastic unit, we can sell these to other countries creating a new export business. This is, I believe a more sustainable and reliable, carbon free energy generation model.

OffGen, who are meant to be regulating electricity generation, employ around 700 people and have totally failed in every aspect of their work. We need to get rid of a lot of regulators and I would start with these cowboys.

Government infrastructure spending should ideally lay a path for private business to come and invest on top of. Like railways, motorways and business parks, infrastructure is an invitation to business to use the new facility to create wealth and innovation. We need some new ideas.

An idea I would put forward is the end of private cars. Possibly all together or at least in major cities and towns. Most cars move so little, off to work or school run and then parked for hours on expensive tarmac covered ground.

The amazing emerging technology like driverless cars just needs someone to commit to it, why not us? Start at the centre and move out. If all cars are banned within central London and many streets are pedestrianised, and some are set aside for driverless car traffic, instead of owning a car, we could user Uber style apps so autonomous cars can pick up people in the most efficient way to make their journey and maximise the car's use. Big out of town car parks would be required as a hubs as well as needing to improve train links that terminate at these hubs.

Lorry deliveries could be charged like a commodity, a big lorry in the middle of the day a high price, small deliveries by the driverless cars, another price, delivery at night, free.

Pollution problem greatly reduced, number of cars massively reduced, car parks turned into living space or green land, streets free from parked cars, half the width of most roads turned over to planting trees and shrubs instead, front gardens re planted, garages converted and crucially, massive investment by private companies building the cars, developing apps and algorithms to control them, doing conversions, roadworks and planting. We could be world leaders as long as we allow competition and innovation. And, on top of all that, imagine how amazing our cities could be without all the cars.

It's going to happen anyway, let it be us rather than Google who make money out of it. Britain has always been good at engineering and design, we have just lacked the ability to implement a large industry from it.

This is an example of the type of visionary idea our country needs. Take an emerging, unstoppable technology and try and make it ours.

Only by creating new wealth at an increased rate can we get our debt burden under control and rebalance our economy.

It's time for change.

## Video 22 - 1 hr 25mins - There is hope.

Youtube search - Documentary about Money and Life, Economics Documentary

https://youtu.be/18LQt_e-OOg?list=PLD7u4sAYcu8qZc2JbDTX_cc28siMUoNOo

Postscript

## The Weaponisation of Words

Just at the end of this book, in defence of words, I would warn you that debate and ideas are being shut down by the weaponisation of words. Politicians and the media have created a false meaning of reasonable words to shut us up.

I mentioned earlier that the word 'exploit' is now used only with its most negative connotations. I may not be a model employer but I told people coming to work for me that I would try to teach them how to maximise their earnings, i.e. to exploit their labour. I think that's a good thing.

To exploit can be amazing, Sit on your arse watching re runs on TV on a Saturday or go out on a bike ride, meet with friends, go kitesurfing. I like to make the most use of my time which is to exploit it for my leisure.

A gallon of petrol can be used in an efficient car for necessary trips or it can be used in a Range Rover for driving half a mile to drop the kids off. To not make full use of petrol is a waste as it hasn't been fully exploited.

Many other words are becoming weaponised, used as a stopper on debate, especially by journalists made lazy by the effectiveness of this weapon. When they are used, they are deployed to show how powerful the journo is, not to get information or debate and they are most often used on the representative of the alternate view.

Words like racist and sexist have become devalued to a state where they mean almost nothing but are useful to end debate.

The Brexit vote was won partly on people's frustration and disgust of being considered 'racist' by the establishment for having concerns about our country's intake of people of different cultures.

Racist, no debate. Sexist, no debate.

Populist is a word we are hearing more now. Another smug media put down for legitimate concerns about the nature of democracy. Voting is meaningless without choice, they vote in China after all. Populist movements only come into being when the established parties FAIL.

Conspiracy is another word being used to help strengthen and entrench the official version of events. "yes, but aren't you just a conspiracy theorist?" the journos will say.

Conspiracy, no debate, fringe loon.

Non news is everywhere. Non news is our diet, no debate, no outsiders, stick to the official line.

## Investment Strategy

I am not qualified to give investment advice but my journey started by trying to find a strategy for investing my pension. It would be remiss if I didn't tell you, broad strokes like, what that strategy will be.

I say 'will be' as we're still waiting for planning permission for a new commercial building that we intend to put up, so our cash is just that at the moment. I have been uninvested since just before the last election.

(For those of you paying attention, you will see that this will put us fully invested in commercial property. As I said, I'm not giving financial advice as any advisor worth their salt would not go all in in one market sector - wish us luck though.)

What I will do when my pension has funds available again is to invest in companies that make money. That shouldn't need saying should it, but in our warped financial system, this ability is often overlooked.

There are four main strategies for investing, no hold on, it's five isn't it.

1. Growth - you buy a share hoping that the herd are on the way because some new whizz bang technology or gold find will boost their interest and then the share price. Not a bad idea but not for me. I want a strategy where I don't have to follow the day to day movements of the share price.

2. Momentum - you buy a share whose price is on the up. Probably the herd is already arriving but if you're in on time, there may still be some growth for you. Hhmmmmm? Not for me, same reason as above.

3. Quality - you buy the big boys, companies with distinguished names and good market share. Solid, dependable, boring? Boring is what I'm looking for, but these companies don't always make that much money. They are heavily bought by the big fund managers to be put into retail funds that form the backbone of most people's pensions. They are sought after shares, the herding effect drives up the price and therefore reduces the yield. Yeahh, boring is good, but low yield sucks.

4. Value - you buy the shares that no one else likes that much, there's no herd. There are two sides to value investing. Contrarian, which means buying a share whose price has dropped a lot on bad news. The herd leaves, the share becomes 'oversold' and if you have the cahoonas, it could be a good time to buy a whole bunch and wait for the herd to come back. Naahhhh, not for me. And secondly, value investors can find good, honest money making companies that don't attract the attention of the herd, have increasing sales, increasing profits and turn profits into cash and dividend. Winner, winner, chicken dinner. That's for me.

How to find these companies.
You will need to do a bit of research or/and cheat like I do.

I use a service called Stockopedia which filters investment information and presents it to you in an easy to digest format. One of the things about this service that I like is that they have lots of different strategies from the financial gurus like Buffet, Slater and Petrovski, and you can make up your own.

I have made my own to find boring, value shares where I can buy, hold and mostly forget. This is what I use to scout contenders.

This is the filter that I built in Stockopedia. The Stockopedia stock and quality ranks are metrics produced by stockopedia's own algorithms.

No net debt = Enterprise value below Market cap.
Market cap over £50 million
Price to Earning ratio less than 15. (no herd)
Stockopedia Quality rank greater than 80.
PEG less than 1.5
Yield greater than 3%
Stockopedia Stock rank greater than 80.

This filter will give me 20 or so shares to consider. I then look through and find the companies that are growing nicely and consistently turn their earnings per share into free cashflow. If there is a funny year in the cash flow, you can normally find and acquisition or other one off cost that has drained the coffers in that year.

Then, I find the company paying the highest dividend and hope to hell the herd finally turns up.

Ohh yes, the late entry into the share buying strategies, the fifth strategy?

5. Gambling - yes, buying any idiotic share that a newspaper, website, blog or telly program waves in front of your face. Looking at charts and guessing which way it will go next. Listening to the news for the masses. Gambling - definitely not suitable for use with your pension.

Printed in Great
Britain
by Amazon